The
Golf Nut's
Book of
Amazing
Feats &
Records

The *Golf Nut's* Book of Amazing Feats & Records

Bruce Nash
and Allan Zullo
with George White

Robson Books

First published in Great Britain in 1996 by Robson
Books Ltd, Bolsover House, 5-6 Clipstone Street,
London W1P 8LE

Copyright © 1994 Nash & Zullo Productions, Inc
The right of Nash & Zullo Productions to be identified
as author of this work has been asserted by them in
accordance with the Copyright, Designs and Patents Act
1988

British Library Cataloguing in Publication Data
A catalogue record for this title is available from the
British Library

Cover design and illustration and all interior illustration
by Mark Anderson

ISBN 1 86105 030 5

Printed in Finland by WSOY

To Ron Ziskin, whose creative strokes of genius place him atop the leader board of TV producers.
　　　　　—Bruce Nash

To Audrae Marzorati, an avid golfer with a habit of standing too close to the ball—after she's hit it.
　　　　　—Allan Zullo

To my brother Jerry, who's no golfer, but the best sport I know.
　　　　　—George White

Contents

For the Record

Golf record books are filled with all sorts of statistical information—average putts per green . . . longest driving distance . . . lowest strokes per round.

What do all these records have in common?

They're *boring*!

Unfortunately for golfers, there has never been a record book to capture the wackiest, zaniest, and most bizarre moments of golf. Until now.

As authors of the Sports Hall of Shame book series and creators of the syndicated "Sports Hall of Shame" comic feature, we have chronicled thousands of wild, crazy, and outrageously funny but true stories. In the following pages, we present such little-known nutty golf records as:

- Most golf balls hit to the green while dancing (12, by Fred Astaire)
- Lowest score playing St. Andrews by the light of the moon (93, in 1876)
- Longest time a pro carried an out-of-bounds stake on the Tour (6 months, by Roger Maltbie)
- Highest-priced cow ever won by a pro ($5,000, by Ian Baker-Finch)
- Highest score deliberately taken for a hole in one (3)

With the help of George White, golf writer for the *Orlando Sentinel*, we interviewed pros on the PGA Tour, the LPGA Tour, and the Senior PGA Tour to get the inside scoop on their most offbeat records. We also combed golf publications such as *Golf Digest*, *Golf*, *Golf Week*, and *Golfworld* for backup material, and we received assistance from golf historian Dawson Taylor.

Although many of these records have never been officially documented, we did our best to verify each one. However, we welcome evidence from readers of records that top the ones we included in this book or of new records that we neglected to compile. Flip to the back of the book to learn how to send your contributions to us. We'd love to hear from you.

One thing is certain. The history of this centuries-old sport boasts a rich heritage of hilarious moments from tee to green.

The
Golf Nut's
Book of
Amazing
Feats &
Records

1

Unbelievable Shots

Highest Handicapper to Hit a Double Eagle Off Another Player's Shoe

18-handicapper
Tommy Thomas, 1990
Redstone Golf Course
Redstone Arsenal, Alabama

Tommy Thomas was about to hit his second shot on the par-5, 497-yard third hole at Redstone Golf Course when he noticed the group ahead of him was on the green putting out.

With an 18-handicap, Thomas, of Huntsville, Alabama, had no delusions of reaching the green in two, so he felt totally safe hitting his second shot. Much to his surprise, he caught the ball as solidly as he had ever hit a 3-wood in his life.

As the ball soared straight and true down the fairway, Thomas watched its flight in wonder . . . and then in consternation. He realized that the ball was actually going to reach the green where Ray Stephenson had just knocked in a putt for a birdie.

Oblivious to Thomas's incoming shot, Stephenson happily walked toward the cup to retrieve his ball. Just then, Thomas's ball landed on the green, smacked into the toe of Stephenson's shoe—and ricocheted right into the hole for an incredible double eagle 2!

Out in the fairway, Thomas didn't know whether to hide or celebrate. Rather than be upset over being hit by another golfer's ball, Stephenson was glad to have lent a hand—or in this case a foot—in achieving such a rare feat.

Said Thomas, "It was the best shot I've ever hit in my life."

First Golfer to Unintentionally Hit an Approach Shot into His Own Pocket

Aubrey Boomer, 1923
St. Anne's Golf Course
Scotland

During a 1923 tournament at St. Anne's Golf Course in Scotland, Aubrey Boomer was playing the eighth hole when he lined up his approach shot.

He swung and lofted the ball straight up in the air, but then lost it in the sun. Neither he nor his playing partners saw the ball land.

After a search of the area around the green failed to find the ball, officials were prepared to hand Boomer a penalty for losing his ball. But then the golfer noticed a solid object in the right-hand pocket of the jacket he was wearing. He reached in—and, to his amazement, produced the missing ball.

Most Yards a Drive Inadvertently Was Hit Backwards

300 yards
Dr. George Russell
1913 Braids Tournament
Scotland

Dr. George Russell walloped a long drive that most any golfer would be proud to hit—except for one thing. He inadvertently hit it backwards!

Playing in the 1913 Braids Tournament in Scotland, Dr. Russell displayed a bizarre backswing. As he got set for a drive off the tee, he accidentally struck the ball on one of his back waggles. The ball jumped the fence behind the tee and careered down a steep hill, coming to rest 300 yards away.

Most Yards That a Drive Reversed Direction

250 yards
Mark Witt
1991 Ben Hogan Knoxville Open

Pro golfer Mark Witt hit the longest "boomerang" tee shot in tournament history.

Witt was playing the Ben Hogan Knoxville Open when he smashed a prodigious drive on the par-4, 375-yard 17th hole at Willow Creek Country Club. His tee shot traveled to within 75 yards of the green where it rolled through the fairway and then onto an entrance road to the golf course.

The uphill angle of the road stopped the ball's forward motion and started it rolling back toward the tee. A stunned Witt watched helplessly as the ball slowly headed closer and closer to where he was standing until, after reversing direction for 250 yards, it died just 50 yards from the golfer.

Witt recovered nicely, however. He took a drop from the pavement, then walloped a 3-wood that landed close enough to the green for him to pitch up and make the putt for bogey.

Most Consecutive Shots That Hit the Same Telegraph Pole

2 consecutive shots
Karl Klinger, 1936
Victoria Golf Club
Cheltenham, Australia

Karl Klinger just wanted to go out and enjoy himself on the golf course. He felt good and thought that perhaps the day would be a memorable one. It was—but not like he had expected.

He started the round shooting extremely well. But then, at the tenth tee, he mis-hit his drive. It sailed off to the left and struck a telegraph pole. The ball bounced back and rolled past the chagrined golfer.

Under the local rules, Klinger was permitted to drop and hit again, which he did. Unbelievably, his second shot hit the exact same pole. Like before, it rebounded toward him. Unlike before, the ball slammed into Klinger's face—and fractured his nose.

Lowest Score Made from a Ball Lodged in a Woman's Bosom

3
Gary Player
1968 World Series of Golf

For Gary Player, it was the most unusual par he ever recorded in tournament play.

At the 1968 World Series of Golf, Player was

locked in a tense duel for the lead when he reached the par-3, 178-yard 12th hole at Akron's Firestone Country Club. He hit his tee shot slightly off line to the right, where the green drops off sharply to a stand of cedar trees. The ball appeared headed for real trouble when it flew into the gallery.

Anticipating the worst, Player marched toward the spot where he last saw his ball. When he got there, however, he was surprised to find a woman with her arms folded across her chest, looking very distressed.

Suddenly, Player realized why she looked troubled. There was his ball—lodged between her arms and her breasts. "I didn't know what to do with the ball," the woman told him. "It just bounced into my arms like this and I froze."

This was a problem that required a rules official. If the woman simply unfolded her arms and let the ball drop to the ground, it would have rolled down the slope and into the trees. The official told her to give the ball to Player, who was then allowed to place it at the woman's feet, at a spot only a few yards from the green.

Player then chipped close to the flag and parred the hole.

The woman proved to be extremely critical to the final outcome of the tournament. Had the ball not landed there, Player might well have made bogey or even double bogey. As it was, he went on to win the tournament in a playoff over Bob Goalby.

And who was the woman who saved Player those vital strokes? None other than Mrs. Mark McCormack—the wife of Player's business manager!

Longest Drive Mis-Hit in a PGA Tour Event

787 yards
Carl Cooper
1992 H.E.B. Texas Open

Never before has a tee shot traveled as far as Carl Cooper's odds-defying drive. It went 331 yards *past* the par-4 green!

Cooper, a struggling 31-year-old PGA Tour veteran, gave new meaning to the term *long shot* during the second round of the 1992 H.E.B. Texas Open at San Antonio's Oak Hills Country Club. Using an oversized driver on the 456-yard third hole, Cooper pushed his tee shot way right. The ball carried about 300 yards before heading on a journey that left pros, caddies, officials, and spectators in awe.

After the ball landed on a paved cart path, it followed the asphalt trail by taking one big bounce after another downhill. To everyone's amazement, the ball bounded down the path past the third green . . . then the fifth green . . . beyond the sixth tee . . . all the way to the 12th green!

It might have rolled to Houston had it not finally plunked into a chain link fence. Cooper's caddie measured the stray drive at a whopping 787 yards! That's nearly a half mile—longer than any par-5 and longer than three normal shots of a good player.

"It was just a freak deal," recalled Cooper, who was 190th on the Tour money list. "I wasn't mad or angry that the ball kept going and going. In fact, I was kind of excited that I had hit it so far. Guys who are great players are winning the Masters and the U.S. Open, but nobody has ever hit one this far."

After being given a drop to clear himself from the fence, Cooper needed a 4-iron and an 8-iron just to get back toward the third green. A chip shot and two putts later, he recorded a double bogey 6. (As cruel fate would have it, Cooper eventually missed the cut—by two shots.)

When the golfer finished the hole, his caddie took the ball and was about to toss it to a spectator when Cooper stopped him and said, "Don't give that ball away. That's the longest ball in the history of golf."

Most Feet Climbed Up a Tree to Retrieve an Errant Shot in a U.S. Open

25 feet
Nick Faldo, 1992
Pebble Beach Golf Links

The par-5, 464-yard 14th hole at Pebble Beach Golf Links is a particularly nasty hole—a narrow dogleg right with a couple of huge oaks guarding the entrance to an elevated green. It was in one of these old seaside trees that Nick Faldo reached the height of embarrassment in his otherwise outstanding career.

On the final day of the 1992 U.S. Open, Faldo mis-hit his 9-iron approach to the green. His ball headed straight into a big oak, but no one saw it come down. So the distinguished British golfer decided to do something most un-British—climb up the tree in hopes of finding his ball.

Faldo started his journey on the lower branches, shaking the limbs at every stop and going successively higher and higher. At one point, the Tarzan-like golfer stopped to yell down to the gallery, "Where the hell is Jane?"

He eventually got up to 25 feet, but he failed to find his ball. Apparently, it was still stuck in the thicker branches above. Faldo eventually had to play a provisional ball and scored a triple bogey 8 on the hole.

After the round, a chagrined Faldo said, "I haven't climbed a tree like that since I was a kid in knee pants."

Highest Score on a Par-3 Hole by a Hall of Famer

11
Ben Hogan
1946 Jacksonville Open

It hardly seems possible that one of the top players of all time could have stumbled so badly at such a short par 3.

But in the third round of the Jacksonville Open at Hyde Park Golf Course, Ben Hogan shot an atrocious 11 on the 150-yard seventh hole.

He had started the day one shot out of the lead and proceeded to par the first six holes. On the seventh hole—which featured a green that was flat on the right side and sloped on the left—Hogan lofted his tee shot purposely toward the left because he wanted to leave himself an uphill putt. He thought he had hit a fine shot.

But the ball hit the green and bounced off, prompting his caddie to say, "Mr. Hogan, I think we are in the lake."

A disbelieving Hogan shot back, "What lake?"

Although he had played the course four times, he wasn't aware of any water on the left side. But then he discovered that trees were shielding the lake from the tee. After searching for his ball, he found it in two inches of water.

Thinking it wouldn't be too difficult to hit it out of the water, Hogan rolled up a pants leg and swatted the ball. It flew out of the water, but struck the bank and trickled back into the drink again.

Again Hogan swung. And again the results were the same. By this time the water had muddied so badly that he couldn't find his ball. So Hogan trudged back to the drop area to play another ball—and launched that one into the lake too.

Eventually he hit a ball onto the green and two-putted for his inglorious 11. He finished the round with an 82 that put him out of the running.

When Hogan returned to his hotel room, his wife Valerie asked him how he had played.

"I told her I had taken an 11 on a par-3 hole," Hogan recalled, "but she didn't believe me.

"We were in a corner room and the windows were open and about that time the voice of a newsboy came floating up. He was shouting, 'Extra! Extra! Ben Hogan takes an 11 on a par-3 hole!'

"Only then did Valerie believe me."

Most Times Being Beaten by an Opponent's Hole-Out

4 times
Greg Norman
1986–90

If ever there's a "Heartbreak Kid" in golf, it's Greg Norman. He's lost four tournaments on the last hole when his opponents holed out incredible shots from off the green. Two of those shots prevented Norman from winning majors.

Norman's first heartbreak happened at the 1986

PGA Championship at Inverness. Norman, who had led almost the entire day, was on the 18th green waiting to putt for an apparent victory. But then, in one of the classic shots in tournament history, Bob Tway blasted his ball into the cup from a greenside bunker to claim the title. No golfer had ever chipped in on the 72nd hole to win a major championship before.

At the very next major, the 1987 Masters, it happened again when Larry Mize holed out during a playoff with Norman. The Shark had put his ball on the 11th green while Mize had missed far to the right. Mize faced a 140-foot chip to a very slick green at a pin cut close to a pond.

"I didn't think Larry would get down in two from there," Norman recalled. "And I was right. Unfortunately, he got down in one."

Norman's heartbreak should have been enough for any mortal to endure, but there was more suffering to follow. At the 1990 Nestle Invitational, Norman was holding a one-shot lead as he stood on Bay Hill's 18th tee. Up ahead of him, in the fairway, Robert Gamez stood with a 7-iron, facing a 176-yard shot over water.

Norman then watched in disbelief as Gamez holed out the fairway shot for a stunning eagle. When Norman couldn't make a birdie, yet another championship was lost on an opponent's dramatic hole-out.

One month later, Norman was victimized by yet another spectacular shot. This time he had just finished making birdie on the difficult 18th hole at the USF&G Classic, pulling into a tie with David Frost. Frost, who had to make par on the final hole to get into a playoff with Norman, looked like he didn't stand a chance when he hit his second shot into a difficult bunker. But Frost belted his ball out of the bunker perfectly and into the cup for an amazing tourney-winning birdie. All Norman could do was shake his head in stunned disbelief.

Of the four, Mize's chip-in was the most difficult pill to swallow "because it came right on the heels of Bob Tway's," Norman recalled. "I would say Larry Mize's position was a hundredfold worse than Tway's. I thought I was totally in control of the situation. Mize was definitely the hardest to take."

Most Strokes Taken by a Foursome in an 18-Hole Round

836 strokes
Angelo Spagnolo (257), Jack Pulford (208), Joel Mosser (192), and Kelly Ireland (179), 1984 TPC at Sawgrass

Can a weekend golfer shoot 179 and be the low player in his foursome—by 13 strokes?

Only if he is the best of the four worst avid golfers in America, as determined by *Golf Digest* magazine, and he is playing one of the toughest courses in the world, the TPC at Sawgrass.

Kelly Ireland had the lowest score of an awfully awesome foursome that, on scout's honor, tried to play their best and shot a woeful combined score of 836. That figures out to an average of 209 for 18 holes, or nearly 12 strokes a hole.

Ireland, 41, a trial lawyer from Tyler, Texas; Joel Mosser, 45, a stockbroker from Aurora, Colorado; Jack Pulford, 48, a restaurant owner from Moline, Illinois; and Angelo Spagnolo, 31, a grocery store manager from Fayette City, Pennsylvania, met at the invitation of *Golf Digest* to decide who was America's worst golfer.

Clearly, it was Spagnolo.

But it wasn't easy to achieve such a shameful title. The foursome accounted for 17 whiffs, 102 balls in the water, 124 penalty strokes, no greens in regulation, and no pars. The best score was a bogey, which happened once, and the next best was a double bogey, which happened eight times.

The golfers' scores were fairly close going into the 17th hole, the famed par-3, 138-yard island green at Sawgrass. There, Spagnolo left the others far ahead.

He took an incredibly pitiful 66 on the hole! He plunked 27 balls into the water, including seven shots that actually hit the green but bounded over into the drink on the other side. Eventually, he had to wave the white flag and putt all the way along the cart path, over the narrow bridge, and onto the green, where he finally got down after three putting. It took the hacker 40 minutes to play the hole.

"After that, the wheels came off a bit," Spagnolo said, explaining why he made 22 on the 18th and final hole.

Meanwhile, Ireland wasn't crowing about being the "medalist" of the four. "I've never seen anything as tough in my life," he said of the course. "On the 11th [a 529-yard par 5], I used every club in my bag—every single one. I was hitting 24 before I got to the fairway."

Longest Time for an Approach Shot to Fall onto the Green

50 seconds (estimated)
Bobby Locke
1936 Irish Open

During the 1936 Irish Open, pro Bobby Locke lofted his tee shot at the 100-yard, par-3 12th hole.

He and the gallery followed the flight path of the ball as it headed straight for the pin. Then everyone waited and waited for the ball to drop onto the green. But there was no thud. In fact, there was no ball. It seemed to have disappeared into thin air.

Members of the gallery looked everywhere around them, but failed to find the ball. One of the marshals peeked into the hole, thinking that perhaps the ball landed in the cup. But the ball wasn't there.

The marshal then leaned on the flagstick. To everyone's surprise, the ball fell out and landed a few inches from the hole. Only then did Locke and the others realize that the ball had become entangled in the flag.

Locke then tapped it in for a birdie.

Most Consecutive Shots in Which a Ball Was Lodged in a Tree

2 consecutive shots
Fred Walker, 1985
St. Jean DeMantha Golf Club
St. Jean DeMantha, Quebec

The trees at St. Jean DeMantha Golf Club have not been terribly kind to Fred Walker of Rawdon, Quebec.

During a forgettable round, Walker hit a shot that stuck in a branch of one of the offending trees. He started to take an unplayable lie, but since the ball was staring at him right at eye level, Walker decided to take a baseball swing at it.

The ball zoomed out of the branches—and made a beeline for another tree 30 yards away. Once again, the ball got snagged in a branch.

Wishing he had a chain saw, Walker dropped a new ball and took an unplayable lie penalty.

Longest Drive by a Senior

515 yards
Mike Austin
1974 U.S. Seniors Open

When pro Mike Austin was 64 years old, he shocked the golfing world by launching what is still the longest drive in Senior PGA Tour history—a 515-yard monster during the 1974 U.S. Seniors Open at the Wildwood Golf Club in Las Vegas.

Aided by a 35-MPH tail wind, the ball soared over the fairway and landed 65 yards past the green on the par-4, 450-yard fifth hole.

In 1993, Austin, who at the age of 82 was still teaching the game five days a week at the Studio City (California) Golf and Tennis Club, recounted his memorable shot: "What I remember is that after chipping back to the green, I three-putted for a damn bogey. But it was one hell of a drive, wasn't it?"

Most Balls Lost While Golfing to the Summit of a Mountain

63 balls lost
Four Aberdeen University students, 1961
Scotland

Four Aberdeen University students looked at Scotland's Ben Nevis and decided it would be a great challenge to reach the top—by golfing there.

Armed with dozens of golf balls, the four intrepid golfers assaulted the 4,406-foot-tall mountain with their trusty golf clubs. Try as they might, they never made it to the top.

The four had to concede victory to the mountain after losing all of their 63 balls. When the end came, they had totalled 659 strokes.

2

Astounding Feats

Most Golf Balls Hit to the Green While Dancing

12 golf balls
Fred Astaire, 1938
Pasadena, California

Although recognized as one of the world's greatest dancers, Fred Astaire was also a fine golfer—and he proved his prowess with both his club and his feet in a remarkable dance scene in the 1938 film *Carefree*.

The script called for Astaire, at a golf club, to dance atop tables and furniture, glide down halls, bound out onto the terrace, and tap his way to the practice range where he was to hit a dozen golf balls while still dancing.

To make the golfing portion of the dance routine—which was shot on a course in Pasadena—more compelling, Astaire and director Mark Sandrich decided to shoot it as one continuous scene. There would be no stopping, no cuts.

The camera started rolling. With music blaring from an outdoor loudspeaker to help him keep a beat, Astaire grabbed a driver and tap-danced his way up to a line of 12 teed-up balls. Moving to the music, Astaire deftly and rhythmically kept dancing while whacking the balls in succession toward a practice green. He didn't miss a beat—or a ball. It was a perfect take.

When some members of the crew went to retrieve the balls, they were astounded at what they saw. All dozen balls were lying on the green—within eight feet of each other!

Coldest Round Ever Played

−27° F
Larry Lujack, 1985
Buffalo Grove Golf Club
Buffalo Grove, Illinois

In weather fit for neither man nor beast, Chicago radio personality Larry Lujack donned arctic gear and played a bone-chilling, teeth-rattling round of golf with the temperature of −27 ° F—and a wind chill of a deadly −75 ° F!

It was bitterly cold in the Windy City when Lujack awakened one Sunday morning in January 1985 and figured he couldn't go another day without a round of golf. He tumbled out of bed and was at nearby Buffalo Grove Golf Club at 7:30 A.M. Obviously he didn't need to call in advance to reserve a tee time.

Bundled in layer after layer of winter survival gear, Lujack trudged for the next five hours in record low temperatures and biting arctic wind while swatting a golf ball around the barren course. With the bulky clothes, it was a little cumbersome to swing the club, but the ball carried well because it bounced on the frozen tundra.

Lujack said he played pretty well, losing just three balls under nearly intolerable conditions. But he wasn't sure what he shot. "The wind blew the scorecard out of my hand on the 13th hole and there was no way I could catch it," he said. "I think I shot between 90 and 95."

When last seen, the scorecard was spiraling toward the east. "It probably blew to Cleveland," he added.

Lujack said he was proudest that he survived without the aid of a single Saint Bernard rescue. "Plowing through deep snow for five hours is tough," he admitted. "When I staggered into the clubhouse, my legs felt like I'd just jogged 200 miles through molasses. I had to lie down."

Most "Shots" Needed to Reach 18 Greens from an Airplane

29 "shots"
Captain Robert Pennington, 1933
Sonning Golf Course
England

RAF pilot Captain Robert Pennington attempted a high-flying form of golf in 1933. He flew 1,000 feet over the Sonning Golf Course, dropping golf balls from his plane, hoping they would land on the greens.

The balls were covered with cloth to minimize bouncing. Pennington needed 29 "shots", or balls, to hit all 18 greens.

Most Countries Played in One Day by a Golfer

5 countries
Simon Clough and Boris Janjic, 1992

Golfers Simon Clough and Boris Janjic played a round of golf in five different countries—in one day!

On June 12, 1992, they played rounds in France, Luxembourg, Germany, Holland, and Belgium.

Clough was an English golf pro at Bossenstein Golf Club in Belgium. Janjic was an Australian pro at Henry-Chapelle Golf & Business Club, also in Belgium. While relaxing at the 19th hole, the two decided to see how many countries they could play in one day. So, with the help of selected golf courses that agreed to give them preferential treatment on the links, Clough and Janjic set out to establish a world record. Attesting to the legitimacy of their odyssey was a member of the Belgian Golfers Union, who acted as an official referee.

At each course, the players golfed as fast as they could—averaging a little more than two hours a round—with their wives riding in carts that carried the clubs. As soon as they finished their round, the pros hopped into their car and zoomed off to the next course in another country.

Amazingly, Clough and Janjic managed to accomplish their feat in 16 hours and 35 minutes—including the time it took to drive the total distance of 273 miles between courses.

For their 90 holes, they had an aggregate score of 772—an average of 77.2 per round each. But if Clough was tired from all that golf and travel, he didn't show it. He set a course record at the final stop.

Lowest Round Shot in Desert Boots

69
Craig Stadler, 1975
Los Angeles Country Club
Los Angeles, California

When Craig Stadler was a member of the University of Southern California golf team, he shared a rental house near the campus with teammate Scott Simpson—who also later turned pro—and three other students.

The guys didn't realize they had forgotten to pay

their utility bill until one day they received a notice from the power company that the electricity would be shut off unless payment was received by noon the next day. The deadline was also the day for USC's golf match with archrival UCLA.

After picking straws, Stadler was the unlucky household member chosen to pay the bill. The next day—clad in an old shirt, slacks, and desert boots—he went to the power company office in downtown L.A. and stood in line for nearly an hour before taking care of the bill. Then he frantically drove across town to the Los Angeles Country Club.

Stadler parked his car, jumped a hedge, and arrived at the first tee with just a minute to spare. In his hurry he left his golf shoes in the car and didn't have time to go back and get them. Still wearing his desert boots, he took three quick practice swings and then started the round.

Apparently, the golf shoes weren't that big a deal—Stadler led his team to victory, shooting a three-under-par 69.

Most Holes Played in a Suit of Armor

18 holes
Harry Dearth, 1912
Bushey Hall
England

An entire round of golf was once played by Harry Dearth, clad in a suit of armor.

In 1912, he accepted a challenge match dressed in full knight regalia. Playing at Bushey Hall, Dearth didn't find it enhanced his play. Instead, he suffered a clanking defeat at 2 and 1.

Longest Drive Hit from the Back of a Pickup Truck

309 yards
George Bell, 1964
Penrith Club
New South Wales, Australia

One of the wackier golf events in Australia is the annual "King of the River" contest in which golfers try to hit a ball across the Nepean River in New South Wales.

In 1964, George Bell climbed into the back of a pickup truck. He teed up a golf ball and swung his two-wood. The ball took off and cleared the river. The carry was certified as a record 309 yards.

No roll was measured. And, no, the pickup wasn't moving, either.

Longest Weekly Round-Trip Commute to Play Golf

550 miles
Tom Harold, 1990–present
Australia

Tom Harold loves golf so much he's willing to go through hell and high water to get to the course.

Most weekends, Harold powers a boat across six miles of shark-infested ocean, motorbikes through more than 250 bumpy miles of Australia's treacherous wilderness, and then drives another 20 miles by car— just to hit the links at the nearest golf course.

It's a harried 550-mile round-trip journey that takes anywhere from 8 to 11 hours each way to complete.

"I'll do anything for a game of golf," said the 35-year-old elementary school teacher, who lives on Goulburn Island, a remote aboriginal community six miles off Australia's northern coast. "It's a pleasant, peaceful, idyllic, tropical setting," he added. "The only thing missing is a golf course."

So on Friday afternoons after school he heads for the closest course—275 miles away in the city of Darwin. With a motorbike in his dinghy, Harold arrives at the mainland after a two-hour boat trip. He pulls out his motorbike, hides his boat under some brush, and then embarks on a grueling seven-hour, 250-mile ride over potholed dirt roads often used by wild boar and buffalo. Harold arrives at a friend's home around midnight, collapsing into bed to rest his jarred spine and weary muscles. On Saturday morning, his friend drives him the final 20 miles to the course.

Harold plays 18 holes on Saturday and nine on Sunday before retracing the arduous trek back home. "The worst part of the round-trip is the final bit— when I have to do the sea crossing to the island in the dark," he said.

"Then, as the waves crash against my boat, I sometimes swear to myself never to make this crazy journey again. But within a few days, as the bruises get less painful, I'm soon craving another game of golf."

Most Brothers to Turn Pro

6 brothers
Mike, Frank, Joe, Phil, Doug, and Jim Turnesa,
1930s and '40s

Never before has any one family produced such a large number of outstanding golfers. The Turnesas—Mike, Frank, Joe, Phil, Doug, and Jim—all played on the PGA Tour during the 1930s and 1940s. However, none of them ever won a major title.

A seventh brother, Willie, bucked the trend and refused to become a pro golfer. Instead, he remained a world-class amateur, winning the U.S. Amateur championship in 1938 and the British Amateur in 1947.

Longest Drive Ever Hit by a Pro off the Eiffel Tower

403 Yards
Arnold Palmer, 1977
Paris, France

Arnold Palmer knew how to make his presence felt in France even if he didn't know how to speak the language. As a publicity stunt in Paris before the 1977 tournament for the Lancôme Trophy, Arnie agreed to tee off from the Eiffel Tower.

He took a sleeve of balls to the second stage of the Eiffel Tower, about 300 feet high, and drove out over the Parisian streets. Palmer's longest drive traveled a record 403 yards.

But Arnie saved his most memorable for last.

His final drive moved right to left before plummeting to the street where it took a big bounce—and landed on the second deck of a moving open-air bus.

Most Holes Played in Formal Attire on One's Wedding Day

18 holes
Captain Gerald Moxom, 1934
West Hill, Surrey
England

Captain Gerald Moxom was addicted to golf. He played whenever he had a free moment, rain or shine. Somehow, he managed to squeeze in time to court a lovely lass in between his army duties and his golf.

When he and his intended set a date to be married, Moxom failed to realize that it fell on the day of the club championship. Too late to change the date of the nuptials, the determined officer wasn't going to let a small matter like a wedding interfere with the tournament.

So after exchanging vows in a quaint chapel in Bournemouth, the bridegroom hustled to his golf club in West Hill, Surrey, in time to tee off in the event. Still dressed in his tuxedo, Moxom shot a round of 61 and won the competition.

Meanwhile, his bride set a record for becoming a golf widow faster than any other wife in England, if not the world.

Longest Drive Ever Hit

2,640 yards
Nils Lied, 1962
Mawson Base, Antarctica

It gets lonely in Antarctica. Hour after hour, there's nothing but cold and snow and penguins. Why, it's enough to make a meteorologist do something crazy, like trying to drive a golf ball across an ice floe!

In 1962, Australian Nils Lied, who was working at the weather station in Mawson Base, decided he wanted to make a name for himself in the golf world. So Lied teed it up outside the compound and looked out over the smooth, frozen ice covering the nearby bay.

Then Lied drove the ball with a powerful swing. The ball sailed in the frigid air, landed on the ice about 225 yards away, and then rolled . . . and rolled . . . and rolled.

The ball finally stopped 2,640 yards away—a gargantuan drive of one and a half miles. No one has ever come close to matching Lied's stupendous drive.

Most Eagles by One Golfer on One Hole

2 eagles
Fred Class, 1974
Lake Venice Golf Club
Venice, Florida

Amateur Fred Class scored two eagles on the same hole—by playing two balls.

Class, of Kitchener, Ontario, accomplished this amazing feat at the Lake Venice Golf Club. Because he was a single on the course, he decided to give his game a little extra work by playing two balls.

At the par-4, 357-yard 11th hole, he hit two outstanding tee shots, both landing within five feet of each other in the center of the fairway. He swatted the first ball with a 9-iron and watched as the ball went into the hole on the fly. He then hit his second ball with the same 9-iron. Remarkably, it was a carbon copy of the first shot. The ball rose into the air and landed right in the hole!

Most Lessons Given by a Teaching Pro in an Average Year

3,000 (estimated)
Ernest Jones, 1924–38
New York

Ernest Jones was the most prolific golf instructor in American history. In his prime, in the 1920s and 1930s, he was averaging 3,000 lessons a year.

Jones was an exceptional English pro who lost his right leg below the knee while in the British army during World War I. He emigrated to the United States in 1924 and became almost as popular as the country's most famous golf instructor at the time, Tommy Armour.

Armour—winner of the U.S. Open, British Open, and PGA Championship—gave about 300 lessons a year. For a fee of up to $100 a lesson, Armour would instruct his wealthy students as he sat under a beach umbrella at the practice range.

Jones's style was totally unorthodox. He did his teaching indoors for no more than $5 a lesson—primarily in a studio that had been a storage room on the seventh floor of a building in midtown Manhattan. He was a classic workaholic, scheduling lessons from 9:30 A.M. to 6 P.M., refusing to stop for lunch. He taught everyone from top executives to secretaries, from lawyers to cab drivers.

Even after he left his classroom, he sometimes wouldn't quit teaching. He was known to give an impromptu free lesson in the rotunda of the Grand Central Terminal while waiting for the train to take him home to Glen Head, Long Island.

If his teaching style was totally unlike almost every other instructor's in America, so was his concept of the golf swing. He didn't dissect the golf swing into parts such as the backswing or the positions of the left arm, knees, and feet. He taught one concept—the swing of the clubhead. He didn't care about form or style. Jones dismissed teaching all the other points of the swing by saying, "If you dissect a cat, you'll have blood and guts and bones all over the place. But you won't have a cat."

3

Odd Tournament Records

Most Golfers Named Bobby Jones in One Tournament

78 Bobby Joneses
Bobby Jones Open, 1992
Cordova Club
Cordova, Tennessee

There's never any doubt who will win the Annual Bobby Jones Open. And there's never any doubt who will finish last. That's because every golfer in the field is named Bobby Jones.

In fact, the only requirement to play in the event is that your name must be Bob, Bobby, Robert, Roberta, or Bobbie Jones. The tournament pays homage to Robert Tyre Jones, the famed golfer who won four U.S. Opens.

"Being a Bob Jones, I wondered how many of us there were," said founder Bob Jones, owner of a computer business in Detroit. "I found four others in the phone book and we had our first tournament in 1979." Ever since word of the tournament spread, Bob Joneses from all over the country and as far away as England and Australia have been teeing up with the Joneses.

The annual event raises money for the Beaumont Hospital, which is dedicated to finding a cure for syringomyelia, a fatal disease that attacks the nervous system. The disease killed the Hall of Fame golfer.

To keep track of all the Bobby Joneses in the tourney, each player has a nickname such as Sandtrap, Computer Bob, Chrysler, and 1992's winner, Iron Man, who beat 77 other Bob Joneses. Famed golf course architects Robert Trent Jones and Robert Trent Jones, Jr., have played. And so have three generations of a family of Bob Joneses from Memphis, nicknamed Banker 1, his son Viking 1, and grandson Viking 2.

Incidentally, the 1992 event was played at the Cordova Club, which was developed by, you guessed it, Bob Jones.

Most Shots Over Par on a Hole After Going to the Toilet in a Major Tournament

3 shots over par
Jack Nicklaus
1978 U.S. Open

Jack Nicklaus was near the lead in the third round of the 1978 U.S. Open when he reached the 13th hole at Cherry Hills Country Club. After hitting his tee shot, he hurried into a nearby portable toilet to answer a very urgent call from nature.

When he came back out, Nicklaus promptly flubbed his shot from the middle of the fairway. He messed up his recovery shot and wound up taking an uncharacteristic seven on the par-4 hole. Thanks to his triple bogey, the Golden Bear quickly faded from contention.

After the round, Nicklaus was beckoned to the media room and asked for an explanation. The superstar coughed a couple of times, looked shamefacedly around the room, then spoke. "I don't know how this is going to look in print, but I never did get my mind back on what I was doing after I went to the toilet."

So, was he sorry that he made the pit stop?

"No," he replied. "I had to go."

Most Topless Dancers Attending a Golf Tournament

30 topless dancers
Forest Creek Golf Course, 1990–1992
Round Rock, Texas

Topless dancers were par for the course during several tournaments sponsored by Austin nightclubs.

In the events, held at nearby Forest Creek between 1990 and 1992, as many as 30 of the clubs' entertainers turned out to spice up the play of the male golfers. Wearing nothing but thong bikini bottoms, the bare-breasted women drove golf carts around the course, served food and drinks, and wrecked the concentration of almost every golfer—none of whom complained.

"It seemed that the more distracted we were, the more tips we gave them," said one golfer.

Beamed a fellow competitor, "We had the breast of both worlds—golf and women."

But residents of Round Rock, which owns the course, teed off against city officials for allowing topless women on the links.

Resident Arvella Goodrum said she was driving by the course when she noticed two women at the eighth tee, obviously missing some parts of their clothing. In fact, from the road, it looked to Arvella like they were missing all their clothes.

"I was shocked," she said. "I turned around and went back to see if I really saw what I thought I saw. The girls were topless, but they did have skimpy little bottoms on."

Mrs. Goodrum and other residents lodged so many complaints that the city council wrote up an ordinance that would prohibit toplessness on the golf course.

Meanwhile, Howard Lennett, manager of Sugar's Uptown Cabaret—one of three topless clubs that sponsored the tournaments—agreed to reevaluate the women's participation in the events. "After all," he explained, "we are concerned about our public image."

Most Holes Played by a Golfer Who Failed to Realize She Was Competing in the Olympics

9 holes
Margaret Abbot
1900 Paris Games

American Margaret Abbot was the first and only winner in women's Olympic golf. She was also the first and only winner who didn't know she was playing in the Olympics!

In 1900, when Margaret was a 21-year-old art student abroad in Paris, the Olympic Committee invited athletes to the Games held in the City of Lights. Among the Olympic medal sports was women's golf.

While growing up in the United States, Margaret had learned the game at Shinnecock Hills and many other courses by playing with her mother, Mary Abbot. The 5'11" Margaret was a decent golfer with a long, sweeping swing and a precise putting touch.

She and her mother were among the 10 women golfers who showed up for the one-round women's Olympic tournament at the Pau Golf Club. Margaret could hardly contain her laughter when she saw her French competitors. They were all dressed with a sophisticated elegance more suited for a night on the town than a day on the links. The Frenchwomen arrived at the club wearing high heels and tight skirts. Incredibly, that's the garb they played in!

Margaret, clad in more traditional, comfortable golf wear, completely outclassed the rest of the field. Not that she was any great shakes with a club. But she was better than all the rest, shooting an 11-over-par 47 to win the nine-hole tourney. Another American, Pauline Whittier, was second, carding a 49.

Years later, Margaret confessed to friends and relatives that she didn't realize she was participating in the Olympics. She played the entire round thinking she was competing in the French Amateur championship. Not until the awards ceremony did it dawn on her that she had competed in the Olympics.

It's hardly surprising that, after such a bizarre beginning, golf was discontinued as an Olympic sport.

Most Holes Played Barefoot at the Masters

18 holes
Sam Snead, 1942
Augusta National

Sam Snead was born and raised in the Virginia mountains at a time and place where shoes were treated in much the same manner as suits—to be worn only on Sundays for church. Snead learned to play golf barefoot, eschewing such fancy trappings as spikes. He even advocated playing shoeless as a great aid in learning proper balance.

At the 1942 Masters, playing a practice round at the revered Augusta National, Snead went the entire 18 holes barefoot. "Shucks," he once said, "I'm really 15 years younger than my birth certificate shows. In Virginia, we don't count the years you go barefoot."

Most Consecutive Tournaments Played Without Winning a Cent

88 consecutive tournaments
Becky Larson, 1985–90

Perhaps a person with less tenacity would have figured that golf was the wrong career. But Becky Larson was going to win a paycheck from an LPGA tournament if it took her a lifetime. Some thought it might.

Larson played five years and 88 tournaments without earning a nickel in winnings. Her moneyless streak finally ended in September 1990, when she made the cut and won $283 at the Rail Charity Classic.

On the most lucrative day of her professional career, after five years of futility, she almost lost her chance to collect!

After finally surviving the cut that virtually assured her of her first payday, Larson had a 10:20 A.M. tee time on Sunday, the final day of the tournament. At the appointed time, however, she was nowhere to be found, so her playing partners teed off without her.

As they were preparing to hit their second shots to the first green, a car came screeching into the parking lot. It was Larson. Still in tennis shoes, she hurdled a fence, sprinted to the tee, and, while still catching her breath, hit her opening drive to prevent being disqualified. Had her partners hit their second shots, she would have been dropped from the tournament and not been able to collect a penny.

As it was, the 29-year-old golfer from Watertown, South Dakota, incurred a two-shot penalty for being late but was allowed to finish the round. Her excuse for nearly blowing her first paycheck? She said she had simply miscalculated her tee time. After all, she hadn't had to play on a Sunday in a tournament in five years.

"It was definitely a bozo move," said Larson, who shot an 80 and finished third from last place. "I would have hated to call my dad and tell him that after finally making a check, I blew it."

Longest Time Between Tournament Victories

12 years, 7 months
Howard Twitty, 1980–93

In 1980, after winning the Sammy Davis, Jr. Greater Hartford Open and finishing the year 14th on the money list, Howard Twitty thought he was at the peak of his career.

Instead, he wallowed in the valley of a victory drought that didn't end until nearly 13 years later, when the 44-year-old veteran captured the 1993 Hawaiian Open by four strokes. He won $216,000— which was more than his combined earnings in any one season with the exception of 1992.

The first person to greet the victor when he came off the green was his daughter, Jocelyn, who was born the same year Twitty had last won. She had never seen her father win a tournament.

"This is very, very special," Twitty said. "There are a lot of emotions, an awful, awful lot of emotions. With my daughter being here to see it, it's one of the special days of my life."

Worst Score for One Hole in European Tour History

20
Philippe Porquier
1978 French Open
La Baule, France

Playing in his first major tournament, Philippe Porquier, a young assistant golf pro, was staying within a few shots of the leaders at the turn of the first round.

But then disaster struck on the 511-yard, par-5 13th hole. Only 40 yards short of the green, Porquier had visions of making a decent chip shot that would set him up for a birdie. He soon lived a nightmare.

He shanked his approach out of bounds. Then he shanked the next two shots. After topping the ball, he shanked two more shots, one of which went out of bounds.

As Porquier was about to play his 13th shot, his caddie planted himself out of bounds so that he'd have an easier time of retrieving the next errant ball. Meanwhile, Porquier apologized to his playing partners for unduly detaining them. Then he swung and shanked . . . swung and shanked.

For his 18th shot, Porquier took aim not at the 13th green, but at the next tee, which was off to the left side of the green. Then he repeatedly told himself, "Do not shank . . . do not shank . . ." When he swung, the ball shanked, darting sideways from his point of aim, and landed on the green ten feet from the cup.

Porquier smiled shyly as the spectators applauded his cunning strategy. Two putts later,

Porquier's name was etched in the record books as the holder of the highest score ever for one hole on the European Tour.

Highest Score Shot in a 36-Hole British Open Qualifier

221
Walter Danecki
1965 British Open

Walter Danecki was a weekend hacker who lacked golfing skills but not gumption. This 47-year-old postal clerk from Milwaukee managed to play in the British Open qualifier!

Danecki had planned a July vacation in England. By chance, he heard he was going to be in the country the same time as the British Open. Suddenly, a light bulb clicked on in his head. Why not do something that would really impress his pals back in Milwaukee? Why not enter the British Open, just to shock his friends who would see his name in the scoring summary for the qualifying event?

And so he sent in his application. Amazingly, the tournament officials accepted it. They reasoned that, although they had never heard of Walter Danecki, he must be a new member of the PGA Tour. With no questions asked, the officials gave him his tee time for the 36-hole qualifier.

Danecki, who seldom broke 100 back in Milwaukee, then went out and shot a dreadful 108-113—that's 71 over par—at the qualifier at Hillside Golf Course in Southport, England.

Tournament officials were not amused when they discovered a duffer in their midst. Talking with reporters after his round, Danecki said, "I can't get into a lot of tournaments in my part of the country, so I thought I would come over here and win a big one. Then they would have to let me in the others."

Best Score of a One-Hole Match Between a Bride and Groom

Bogey 6 (tie)
Christyne Curley Velez and Bill Velez, 1992
Sterling Farms Golf Club
Stamford, Connecticut

To kick off their wedding reception, bride Christyne Curley Velez, a 31-handicapper, challenged her new husband, Bill Velez, a 26-handicapper, to a one-hole match on the par-5, 515-yard 18th hole at Sterling Farms Golf Club.

The wedding guests cheered the newlyweds as they headed for the tee. Still wearing her floor-length chiffon wedding gown and wielding her Big Bertha, Christyne banged her tee shot 175 yards down the right side of the fairway. Velez, wearing tux and tails, outgunned her by 25 yards with a 200-yard drive.

Christyne eventually reached the back fringe of the green in four shots, then nearly got her par when her chip shot struck the flag and bounced a few inches from the hole. She made a bogey 6—and put the pressure squarely on the groom, who was languishing in a greenside bunker in three shots.

Bill, though, managed to extricate himself with a blast that put the ball onto the green in 4, 30 feet from the hole. Now came the big question: Would he nail the long putt and upstage his wife only minutes after exchanging their wedding vows? Or would he do the gentlemanly thing and three-putt, making the

new missus happy in his first official act as a husband?

Bill did neither. Instead, he knocked his first putt
29 feet and then made the one-foot tap-in for a bogey.

The newlyweds had tied not only the knot but
also the match.

Most Consecutive Rounds a Major
Tournament Winner Shot the Same Score

4 consecutive rounds
Denny Shute
1933 British Open

Playing in the Open at St. Andrews, Scotland, Denny
Shute won in a playoff over American Craig Wood.
Shute's regulation four rounds, though, may have
been even more noteworthy than his championship.
Shute recorded the same tally all four days, 73-73-73-
73, for a 292 total.

Most Miles a Pro Rode on the Back of a
Harley to Make a Tournament Tee-Off
Time

3 miles
Gary Player, 1980
Akron, Ohio

Gary Player almost didn't make it on time to the third
round of the 1980 World Series of Golf.

Driving a courtesy car himself, Player left his
downtown Akron hotel at what he thought was plenty
early to make his tee time at the Firestone Country

Club. But the traffic was a terrible mess. Three miles from the course, cars were at a standstill. Player nervously looked at his watch and saw he had only 25 minutes until his name would be called on the first tee.

The diminutive South African, a physical fitness fanatic, calculated it would take him 18 minutes to run the three miles, which would give him seven minutes to catch his breath before he had to tee off. So he abandoned his car at the side of the road and started to run.

Player had gone only a few yards when he spied a group of black-jacketed motorcyclists. He hurriedly approached them and offered to fill the gas tanks of all the cycles if one of them would take him to the course.

"Jump on, man," said the leader, an overweight, bearded biker, as he revved up his high-handlebarred Harley-Davidson. The desperate golfer, who had never been on a motorcycle before, hopped on. Clutching the biker's jacket, Player roared off on the ride of his life.

Twice they were stopped by Akron police as they weaved through traffic and drove on the wrong side of the road. Twice Player talked his way out of a ticket. With a few minutes to spare, the bike reached the gate at Firestone.

"A guard put his hand up to stop us," Player recalled, "but I waved at him and told the driver to keep going." The biker finally screeched to a stop in front of the locker room, much to Player's relief. The two settled on a fee of $20 for the frenzied ride.

"Imagine," said Player who shot a 3-under-par 69 for the round. "Only $20. Why, he had long greasy hair and a big beard, and I could have kissed him."

Most Strokes Improved After Overcoming a Case of the Nerves in One's First Major Tournament

9 strokes
Hal Sutton
1981 U.S. Open

As the reigning U.S. Amateur champion, Hal Sutton was invited to play in his first U.S. Open in 1981 at Merion Golf Club in Ardmore, Pennsylvania.

Nervous beyond belief just to be there, the 23-year-old rookie turned into a human blob of Silly Putty because he was playing with his all-time favorite golfer, Jack Nicklaus. "Jack's been my idol ever since I was a junior golfer," Sutton recalled. "I was paired with a guy I idolized all my life and I was petrified, to tell you the truth. He was the next thing to God."

Shaking and sweating, Sutton started the day with a triple bogey, and things didn't improve much over the next several holes. In fact, after seven holes, Sutton was a pitiful eight over par.

Writhing in embarrassment, the young golfer finally summoned up the courage to speak to Nicklaus. "Did anyone ever tell you how intimidating you can be?" Sutton asked.

Nicklaus smiled and replied, "I'm just as nervous as you are, Hal. The only difference is I've got 20 years of experience in controlling it."

Sutton smiled back, and suddenly the enormous pressure he felt began to ease. He began to play like he had in the U.S. Amateur, hitting one crisp shot after another. In a dramatic turnaround, he mastered the last 11 holes of the round, playing them in an impressive one under par. Unfortunately, he still missed the cut with a seven-over-par 78.

"I was an amateur then and I wanted to play like a pro," Sutton recalled. "I never wanted to be put in that position again. I figured I would either get completely out of the game or completely into the game."

Sutton turned pro, and two years later won his first major, the 1983 PGA Championship.

Worst Score for a Hole in a Major Tournament After Missing a Birdie Putt

9
Tommy Nakajima
1978 British Open
St. Andrews, Scotland

Among the contenders in the third round of the 1978 British Open at St. Andrews, Tommy Nakajima was putting for a birdie three from 30 feet away on the 17th hole. He tapped his putt and then watched in dismay as the ball rode the break of the green and trickled off into the feared Road Bunker.

Once, twice, three times, he tried to blast out of the sand with no luck. "That bunker was so deep and the side was so steep, it was like a wall," he recalled. "I was so mad."

Finally, on his fourth recovery attempt, he made the green and then two-putted to close out a golfing horror for ever known as "The Sands of Nakajima". He was too stunned to believe it. Moments earlier, he was putting for a birdie three; now he had staggered off the green with a shocking nine.

Highest Score in a Tournament by the Course Architect

80
Ben Crenshaw
1991 Kapalua International

Ben Crenshaw learned a humiliating lesson: you shouldn't design a golf course that you can't master.

Crenshaw teamed with Bill Coore in designing the Kapalua Plantation Course on the Hawaiian island of Maui. The course was finished just in time to host the Kapalua International, an event in which most of the players shot excellent scores the first time they played it.

Crenshaw wasn't one of them. Playing on his own course in tournament competition, he shot a woeful seven-over-par 80.

49

Youngest Female to Beat Bobby Jones

12 years old
Alexa Sterling, 1908
Atlanta, Georgia

Alexa Sterling was the only female ever to beat the great Bobby Jones. She was just 12 years old! But then, Bobby was only six.

In 1908, the two friends attended a neighborhood party in Atlanta where they were pitted against each other in a six-hole golf competition. The prize for the winner was a small trophy.

Alexa won the match. But Bobby ended up with the trophy. That's because he ran off with it and took it to bed with him that night.

4

Incredible
Holes in One

Most Balls Hit in One Day While Trying to Make an Ace

1,817 balls
Harry Gonder, 1940

Harry Gonder, an American professional, desperately wanted to make a hole in one. So he went out one day in 1940 and tried his hardest. He believed that if he stood at a par-3 tee and hit one ball after another, he was bound to score an ace.

After arriving at a par-3, 160-yard hole, Gonder started flailing away. For 16 grueling hours, he whacked the same shot over and over, hitting more than 100 balls an hour, from sunup to sundown.

But, sadly, not one went into the hole.

His closest shot came on his 1,756th try. The ball headed straight for the flag, took a bounce on the green, rolled directly toward the hole—and died just an agonizing inch from the cup. The devastated Gonder hit another 61 shots, but, discouraged and fatigued, he called it a day after clubbing 1,817 balls.

The National Hole-in-One Foundation calculates a golfer will make an ace every 12,000 tee shots. If those odds had held for Gonder, he would have had to repeat his efforts for another 5½ days before finally scoring his ace.

Highest Score for Shooting an "Ace"

9
Lew Cullum, 1967
Yacht Club Estates Golf Club
St. Petersburg, Florida

Amateur Lew Cullum had to mark down a 9 on his scorecard—for shooting an "ace"!

Cullum, of Largo, Florida, encountered a world of problems on the par-3, 145-yard 11th hole at Yacht Club Estates Golf Club. It started with a flubbed tee shot into the lake surrounding the hole. Then he sent another drive into the drink. And another . . . and another.

On his fifth try, his tee shot cleared the lake, landed neatly on the green—and rolled right into the cup for what would have been an ace had he hit it on his first attempt.

But because of the stroke and distance penalties from his first four errant drives, Cullum ended up shooting a hole in nine.

Most Holes in One on Consecutive Days by a Blind Golfer

2 holes in one
Margaret Waldron, 1990
Long Point Golf Course
Amelia Island, Florida

Although she was legally blind, 74-year-old Margaret Waldron of Jacksonville, Florida, did what many low-handicap golfers with perfect vision have never done—scored a hole in one.

And if that wasn't incredible enough, she aced the same hole the next day—with the same club and the same ball!

Experts have computed the odds against an amateur scoring a hole in one at 12,000 to 1, and no one yet has attempted to establish the likelihood of a blind golfer recording an ace. "To do it twice on the same hole, two days in a row, using the same club and the same ball, makes the odds beyond comprehension," said Long Point golf pro Ed Tucker.

Waldron had lost her vision 10 years earlier to an eye disease. Instead of giving up sports, though, she continued to be an active golfer, relying on her husband, Pete, to line her up and to describe the hole, distance, and playing conditions.

During a round with friends on March 18, 1990, Pete handed Margaret a 7-iron and pointed her toward the flag on Long Point's 87-yard seventh hole. "I hit the ball solidly," Margaret recalled. "One of my friends said, 'Good hit, Margaret. . . . Wow! Its going for the green! It's going toward the hole!'

"Another friend shouted, 'You've got a hole in one!' We all hugged and I felt a great sense of fulfillment. That night, Pete and I celebrated."

When Margaret arrived at the same hole the next day, she took the same 7-iron and once again hit the 87-yard shot perfectly. The ball rolled into the cup for another ace. "When we went back to the clubhouse, I was so proud," Margaret said. "I don't consider myself handicapped. I am challenged to do the best I can with what I have. What else should I do? Sit home and knit? Not me!"

Most Aces in the Same Cup with the Same Ball on the Same Day

2 aces
Jim Whelehan, 1992
Heather Glen Golf Links
Myrtle Beach, South Carolina

On March 1, 1992, Jim Whelehan turned a routine golf outing into one of the rarest days in links history.

On that day, Whelehan, a phone company executive from Rochester, New York, made two holes in one—in the same cup and with the same ball!

Whelehan, 43, a 5-handicapper, was on a golfing vacation at Heather Glen Golf Links, a 27-hole layout in which some holes are used twice. For example, the par-3, 115-yard fourth hole in the first round doubles as the 13th hole in the second round. This was the hole that Whelehan "owned."

Using a 7-iron in the first round, Whelehan lofted his tee shot onto the green and watched it bounce right into the cup for an ace. As if that wasn't thrilling enough, he hit an identical shot with the same club in his second round of the day for another hole in one. "I'm glad I hit good shots both times," he said. "I didn't knock them in off a rake or run them through a sand trap."

Golf Digest, which has logged unusual hole in one stories since 1952, calculated the odds of the feat at one in a million. Added Whelehan, "I believe that good shots end up one foot from the hole and lucky shots go in. I think it was more good fortune than skill."

Most Objects Hit en Route to a Hole in One

4 objects
Ted Barnhouse, 1981
Mountain View Country Club
John Day, Oregon

Amateur Ted Barnhouse hit one of the wackiest aces in golf history. It ricocheted off four objects before plopping into the cup.

It all happened on the par-3, 145-yard fourth hole at Mountain View Country Club in the little Oregon town of John Day where Barnhouse, a cattleman, played most of his golf.

His bizarre ace began with an awful-looking tee shot—a shank that screamed to the right, sailed over a barbed wire fence, and headed into a herd of cows. The ball smacked into the forehead of a startled bovine, then bounced back toward the course.

The shot next hit a sprinkler head, which redirected the ball over the green and into the third object on its zany journey—a parked lawn mower. From there, the ball ricocheted back onto the green and rolled straight for the flagstick. After banging into the pin—the fourth object—the ball dropped into the cup for a crazy hole in one.

Strangest Award for Acing a Hole

Half a car
Art Schmuckal, 1986
Elmbrook Golf Club
Traverse City, Michigan

Art Schmuckal won half a car because he opened his big mouth seconds before scoring a hole in one.

He and his friend Gil McHuron were playing partners in a tournament at Elmbrook Golf Club—an event that offered a new car to anyone who could ace the 170-yard ninth hole.

When they reached number nine, Schmuckal turned to McHuron and suggested that if either aced the hole, they would share the car. His pal agreed. It seemed a harmless remark, especially since Schmuckal had been playing for 25 years without ever scoring an ace.

But there's a first time for everything, and this time the odds finally caught up with Schmuckal. Using his 4-wood off the tee, he knocked the ball into the cup. He jumped up and down, thinking he had won a brand-new car. But then Schmuckal suddenly realized he owned only half a car because of the agreement he had struck with his friend.

"A deal's a deal," said Schmuckal. So, after figuring out the worth of the car, he bought the other half from McHuron. Said Schmuckal, "The front half was already mine, so I bought the back half."

Most Times Scoring a 3 on an "Ace" in One Month

2 times
John Gentile, 1991
Fountaingrove Country Club
Santa Rosa, California

Amateur John Gentile experienced one of the strangest months in golf history in May 1991.

Playing the par-3, 127-yard fifth hole at Fountaingrove Country Club, Gentile mis-hit a tee shot that veered deep into the rough. Assuming it was lost, Gentile teed up a provisional ball, swatted it, and watched in wonder as it hit the green, bounced once, and settled into the cup. But instead of a hole in one, he had to mark down a 3 as the rules required.

Two weeks later, at the same course, Gentile was teeing off on the par-3, 171-yard 12th hole with his 5-iron. But he lifted his head as he swung, topping the ball about 10 feet in front of the tee. So he took a mulligan.

His next tee shot was perfect, bounding into the cup for his second hole in one of the month. Yet, for the second time, he had to score his ace a 3.

Around the clubhouse, Gentile quickly gained an unwanted reputation. Lamented the golfer, "It's hard being known as the guy who can't do it right on the first shot."

Most Objects Hit En Route to a Hole in One by an Englishman

3 objects
John Remington, 1959
Cotswold Hills Golf Club
Cheltenham, England

There are lucky holes in one that skip through a greenside bunker and pop into ·the hole. And there are those perfectly hit shots that fly straight into the cup without ever touching a blade of grass. However, none will match the wacky, unbelievable ace that was hit by John Remington.

Remington was playing the par-3 seventh hole with a five-iron. A mid-handicapper who had never aced a hole in his life, he had no reason to believe he would record a hole in one.

His tee shot turned into a wild snaphook that whistled toward a drainage ditch to the left of the fairway. Then the ball took a remarkable journey. First, it ricocheted off a drainage pipe and skittered across the grass toward the greenside bunker, where it bounced off a rake. Then the ball popped onto the green and began rolling straight toward the ball of Remington's playing partner. Amazingly, Remington's ball glanced off the other ball—and plopped right into the hole for an incredible ace.

Most Generations of a Family to Ace the Same Hole

3 generations
The Fribley family, 1971–91
Pana Country Club
Pana, Illinois

To the Fribley family, scoring a hole in one on the seventh hole at the Pana Country Club has become a tradition. Three generations of the clan have aced it.

In 1971, 65-year-old John Fribley was the first in the family to conquer the par-3, 186-yard hole with a 3-wood. Four years later, his 16-year-old grandson, Scott, who played on the Pana High School golf team, aced the hole. It took 16 years before another member of the family duplicated the feat. In 1991, Judge Joseph Fribley—John's son and Scott's father—used his 4-iron to become the third generation of Fribleys to score a hole in one on lucky number seven.

Longest Roll of a Dead Ball Jolted into the Cup by an Earth Tremor for an Ace

2 inches
Morton Shapiro, 1956
Indian Springs Country Club
Marlton, New Jersey

Morton Shapiro scored an ace thanks to a rare natural phenomenon.

Shapiro, an attorney from Camden, New Jersey, was playing the 130-yard fifth hole at Indian Springs Country Club when he hit his tee shot with considerable backspin.

The ball landed several yards beyond the cup,

but bit into the turf and spun back. As the ball rolled closer and closer toward the hole, Shapiro was all set to jump for joy over his first ace ever. But to his dismay, the ball died just short of the cup by a couple of inches.

Shapiro stood still on the tee, hoping against hope that the ball would, by some miracle, start up again and plunk into the cup. But there seemed no chance of that happening. The ball had definitely stopped. And there was no wind to gently push it into the hole.

As Shapiro headed toward the green, he walked down a swale that momentarily blocked his view of his ball. By the time he could see the hole once again, he was shocked—his ball wasn't there. He hurried to the cup and to his great surprise found the ball inside. By some miracle, the motionless ball got going again and finished the last two inches of its journey into the cup for a hole in one!

Upon further investigation, it appeared that Mother Nature had lent a hand in the ace. About a minute after Shapiro had teed off, the area was hit with a rare earth tremor. The ground shook just enough to start the ball rolling again right into the hole.

Most Number of Sevens Linked to a Hole in One

7
Kent Averett, 1977
Painted Hills Golf Club
Salt Lake City, Utah

The number seven played a big role in the hole in one made by Kent Averett of Cedar City, Utah, at a par-3, 197-yard hole at Painted Hills Golf Club.

It happened on the seventh day of the seventh month of 1977 (7-7-77 if you're keeping the date numerically). Averett made his ace at the seventh hole—at exactly 7:00 P.M. There was a seventh seven linked to his ace. It was the seventh hole-in-one of the year at Painted Hills.

There could have been more sevens if fate had really wanted to have fun. Averett didn't use a 7-iron; he used a 6-iron. And he didn't shoot a 77 that day; he shot a 72. If only he had been drinking a 7-Up before the shot. . . .

Shortest Time Between Dreaming of Scoring an Ace While Playing with a Dead President and Actually Making One

2 months
Vicki Tanigaki, 1989
Sweetwater Country Club
Sugar Land, Texas

Vicki Tanigaki, a 15-handicapper, dreamed that the late John F. Kennedy had invited her to play golf with him and that during their round, she sank a hole in one.

When she awakened the next day, Vicki went straight to the Sweetwater Country Club near Houston and joined the "Hole-in-One-Club." (Members pay $5 to join. It's like an insurance policy. If a member scores an ace, he or she doesn't have to buy drinks for everyone. The club ponies up the money instead.)

Two months later, Vicki played in her first official tournament at the club. And her dream came true—at least part of it. On the par-3, 150-yard seventh hole, Vicki knocked in a hole in one!

Although Kennedy wasn't there, perhaps his spirit was. The name of the tournament was the President's Cup.

Highest Score Deliberately Taken for a Hole in One

3
Ev Hanlon, 1965
Avon Country Club
Avon, Connecticut

Ev Hanlon had his fill of holes in one by the time he made his third ace in 1965 at Avon Country Club. After each of the first two, he had dutifully endured golf's time-honored tradition of the ace-maker buying a round of drinks for all those in the club bar.

It was a tradition that he didn't want to experience again.

So after his 170-yard tee shot on the 11th hole went into the cup for an ace, Hanlon stunned his playing partners by declining their congratulations. He plucked his ball out of the cup and announced to the group that he was declaring an unplayable lie and taking a penalty stroke. Then he proceeded to place the ball a few feet from the cup and tap it in. "Give me a three," he said.

Hanlon, a district engineering manager, explained that he felt there were far better uses for money than splurging it on drinks for the gang. "I'd rather see it go to some kind of charity, or perhaps a caddie scholarship."

Most Holes in One by an Armless Golfer

8 holes in one
Jim Taylor, 1986–present
Golf Green Golf Center
Longview, Washington

Jim Taylor has hit an incredible eight aces—even though he has no arms!

Taylor, an insurance executive, lost both arms in a childhood accident when he grabbed a 7,000-volt power line while climbing on a roof. Since then, he has used artificial arms and hooks for hands.

He took up golf in 1986, using special rubber bands to help him clasp the club. "At first it was frustrating," he told reporters. "Imagine trying to hold a golf club and not feel it, then swing your whole upper body to force the club in an arc. My friends said I should find an easier game. But I've never been a quitter and I vowed to play, arms or no arms."

Three years later, at the Golf Green Golf Center in Longview, Washington, Taylor drained his first ace. "I never thought I would see a hole in one in my life—and now I'd shot one with hooks instead of hands," he said. "When I got back to the clubhouse, the word had spread and I became an instant local celebrity."

Since then, Taylor has knocked in seven more aces, confirmed Skip Manke, the pro at the golf center. "Jim plays a great game of golf," said Manke. "He just happens to have no arms."

Most Unofficial Aces Scored in One Day

2 unofficial aces
John Murphy, 1982
Wil-Mar Golf Club
Raleigh, North Carolina

It was as though it had never happened.

In one memorable day, amateur John Murphy knocked two tee shots into the cup. But as far as the official rules of golf are concerned, he didn't score an ace either time.

The rules state that for a hole in one to be official, the shot must be witnessed by someone other than the golfer who made it. And it must come during an 18-hole round.

While playing a round by himself one day in 1982 at the Wil-Mar Golf Club, Murphy holed his tee shot at the 175-yard fifth hole. But because he was alone, Murphy knew the unwitnessed ace was not official.

So after he finished the round, Murphy recounted his bittersweet feat to Wil-Mar assistant greens superintendent Hank Grady and then took him back out to the fifth hole. There, the golfer put his tee into the ground and tried to demonstrate what had happened a few hours earlier.

Wonder of wonders, the ball landed in the cup again! But Murphy's joy was short-lived when he realized that this ace wasn't official either because he had played only one hole, and there wasn't enough time to complete a full round.

5

Wild Betting Records

Most Pros Photographed Dropping Their Pants at the Same Time

4 pros
Jack Nicklaus, Arnold Palmer, Gay Brewer, Dave Hill
1973 Ryder Cup

It's one of the most treasured photographs in golf. Nicklaus, Palmer, Brewer, and Hill—all members of the 1973 U.S. Ryder Cup team—had their posteriors snapped for posterity.

It was all the result of a boast made by teammate Lee Trevino. Before his match on the Ryder Cup's final day against Peter Oosterhuis—the number-one player on the European Tour and the favorite—Trevino pledged, "If I don't beat that Peter Oosterhuis, I'll kiss the rears of every member of the team."

Unfortunately, Trevino didn't win. He and Oosterhuis halved the match. But the Americans won the Cup anyway, 19–13, so they were in a mischievous mood when they all convened in the locker room at Scotland's Muirfield Golf Club.

One by one, they challenged Trevino to carry out his promise. They even brought in a photographer to record the event. The photo, guarded now in a private collection, shows Trevino seated, doubled up in laughter.

Nicklaus is removing his pants. Next to him is Palmer, doing the same thing. Brewer, wearing the team blazer, has already doffed his trousers, daring Trevino to pucker up. Dave Hill also has dropped trou.

Did Trevino ever follow through on his pledge? You can't tell from the picture . . . and, publicly, he won't tell anyone.

Fewest Shots Made to Reach a Target
Three Miles Away

32
Freddie Tait, 1898
England

Freddie Tait, Scotland's premier golfer at the turn of
the century, bet friends he could play from the clubhouse at England's Royal St. George's Golf Course to
the one at Royal Cinque Ports Golf Club—a distance
of three miles—in 40 shots or less.

There were two conditions. He could tee each
shot, but he had to use a gutta percha. The gutty—
fashioned out of a gummy substance from India with
a hard billiard ball–like cover—was not known for its
distance.

Nevertheless, Tait succeeded in dramatic fashion.
He reached the grounds of Cinque Ports in only 31
strokes and let fly with his 32nd shot directly at the
clubhouse. The ball shattered a window, signaling
Tait the winner of the bet.

Longest Distance Competitors Played
Apart from Each Other

9,000 miles
English and Australian golfers, 1957

The first known golf match by telephone was
played in 1957 when the Cotswold Hills Golf Club
of Cheltenham, England, challenged the
Cheltenham Golf Club of Melbourne, Australia.

The match was open to every member of both
clubs and the aggregate score was phoned in to
England. It was a close match. Cotswold beat
Cheltenham, 564–570.

Fewest Strokes Needed to Golf from Ceres, Scotland, to the 18th Hole at St. Andrews

236 strokes
R.S. Little, 1938

A pair of students at St. Andrews University tried to outdo each other in a wacky contest.

They teed off at Ceres, an inland Fifeshire village, and clubbed their golf balls until they arrived at the 18th hole on the Old Course at St. Andrews, nine miles away.

The competitors, R.S. Little and K.G. Sherriff, had set some ground rules. Each used just one club and the ball could be teed up before each shot. The final rule: it would be no contest if one of them did not hole out in less than 300 strokes. Both golfers managed to complete the event under the limit.

After eight hours of competition, a pace better than a mile per hour, Little prevailed by two strokes, defeating Sherriff 236 to 238.

Fewest Shots Made in a Round by a Golfer in Full Battle Gear

94 shots
Nigel Farrar, 1914
Royston Links
England

While his fellow soldiers groused about the weight of their cumbersome battle gear, Nigel

Farrar called them "sissies" and said it was no big deal to wear the equipment.

In fact, Farrar boasted, he could play a round of golf in less than 100 strokes while in full battle gear. Several soldiers took him up on the bet.

In 1914, just before World War I broke out, Farrar donned his full infantry gear, complete with water bottle, field kit and haversack. Then he attacked the Royston Links. He won the wager by shooting a 94.

Fewest Strokes Needed to Golf from Tower Bridge to White's Club

142 strokes
Richard Sutton, 1939
London

Stockbroker and avid golfer Richard Sutton played out his fantasy of a cross-city golf excursion in London in 1939.

Sutton made a wager of £100 that he could play from Tower Bridge across town to White's Club on St. James Street in fewer than 200 strokes.

Using only a putter, Sutton whacked the ball along Southwark Bridge across the Thames without hitting the ball into the water. Then he belted away, along the streets and through the park. Sutton easily won the bet by making it to White's Club in only 142 strokes.

Fastest Round in Dense Fog Without Losing a Ball

2 hours, 15 minutes
John Ball, 1907
Hoylake Golf Course
England

John Ball, England's leading amateur player at the time, arrived at Hoylake near Liverpool one day when fog made it impossible to see the flagstick from the edge of the green.

Other golfers decided it wasn't worth the hassle of hunting all day for golf balls in the thick soup. Ball contended they were wimps. So one of them presented him with a sporting wager that he quickly accepted.

To win the bet, Ball had to play 18 holes at Hoylake in less than 2½ hours, break 90, and play the entire round with the same ball.

He won the bet, zipping around the fog-shrouded course in 2 hours, 15 minutes, and shooting an 81. And he did it without losing a ball. That's because before teeing off, he had painted his ball black!

Lowest Score Shot by a Golfer Who Predicted the Results

64
Joe Ezar, 1936
Sestriere Golf Club
Sestriere, Italy

Joe Ezar, one of the game's most colorful hustlers and trick shot artists, won a hefty wager when he broke a course record just as he predicted he would.

In the town of Sestriere, site of the Italian Open the following week, Ezar met the president of the Fiat Motor Company on the golf course. The two were exchanging boasts about their linksmanship when Ezar claimed he could tie the course record of 66 the next day.

"I'll bet you 5,000 lira that you can't match it," said the auto bigwig.

"And if I break the record with a 65?" asked Ezar.

"I'll double it."

"And how much would a score of 64 be worth?" the golfer queried.

"Forty thousand lira," came the reply.

"I'll tell you what I'll do," Ezar said. "Before I play the round, I'll write down the score I'll make on each hole for my 64."

After jotting down his hole-by-hole predictions, Ezar headed straight to the bar where he drank away most of the night. Were it not for a very persistent caddie who dragged him out of bed the next morning, the besotted Ezar would never even have made it to the course.

With a camel hair coat draped around his shoulders, Ezar staggered to the first tee. Despite bleary eyes, shaky hands, and wobbly legs, he golfed with the consummate skill of a Bobby Jones. Incredibly, Ezar played the first eight holes exactly as he had predicted.

He slipped on the ninth hole, making a 4 where he had predicted a 3. But he made up for it on the next hole by sinking a birdie putt for a 3 instead of the 4 he had forecast.

Ezar then matched his predicted scores for the last eight holes and broke the course record by shooting a 64—just as he said he would.

The hung-over hustler pocketed the 40,000 lira and promptly went back to the bar to celebrate.

Most Strokes an Amateur Gave a U.S. Open Champion in a Round

2 strokes
Bobby Jones, 1928

Tommy Armour won the U.S. Open at Oakmont Country Club near Pittsburgh in 1927—a tournament where the legendary Bobby Jones played poorly. Jones finished in a tie for 11th, unthinkable for him in that era. But both golfers knew that Jones was the better player.

In the summer that followed, Armour and Jones, who were close friends, played numerous friendly matches for small wagers. Armour never won.

Jones was embarrassed by taking money from a professional whose friendship he valued so highly. So he began discreetly giving Armour strokes in their matches—one a side.

Jones's sporting gesture would never have been known had not Armour himself told the story later in life. Jones never mentioned it to a soul, but Armour had no problem confessing that he couldn't beat Jones without an "equalizer."

Asked how a Tour pro could accept "ups" from an amateur, particularly when the pro was the reigning U.S. Open champion at the time, Armour bristled, "because that's how goddamn good Bobby was."

Most Money Won on the Golf Course by an Army Private While Trying to Get Home

$45
Chi Chi Rodriguez, 1959
Fort Dix Golf Course
Fort Dix, New Jersey

While Chi Chi Rodriguez was in special services in the Army, he won the post's golf championship at Fort Sill, Oklahoma. By the time he was due to be discharged, his golf game was nearing Tour caliber.

Chi Chi was sent to Fort Dix, New Jersey, for the official mustering out. He hoped to fly home to Puerto Rico, but there was this rather urgent matter of funds. He only had $45 in his pocket and the plane ticket cost $55.

He wandered over to the golf course, where he knew he might be able to hustle enough money to buy a ticket home. By chance, the Fort Dix post champion was on the course and Chi Chi talked him into a friendly wager.

"I told him I'd stand on my head, and whatever fell out of my pockets, I'd play for," Chi Chi recalled. "I needed $55 dollars for the plane fare. He was a sergeant and I was a PFC weighing 117 pounds. If I lost, I would have had to stay on the base and pull kitchen duty for who knows how long."

Needing desperately to win so he could go home, Rodriguez played one of his best games up to then. "I birdied the first five holes and won," he said. "I collected my money and made the plane."

Lowest Score Ever Shot by a Pro to Win a Bet

57
Orville Moody, 1979
Bowie Country Club
San Antonio, Texas

In 1979, pro Orville Moody wound up in a small-stakes gambling match with some of the locals at San Antonio's Bowie Country Club. He proceeded to have one of the best golfing days of his life, shooting a stunning 57.

"The course was only about 6,300 yards [in length]," he recalled. "But I made three eagles. Hey, you've got to hit some good shots to shoot 57 on a par-72 course. I don't care how short it is."

When the round was over, some of the skeptics told Moody that he really wasn't that good. They said it was a fluke or pure luck. It was, they contended, something besides just incredible talent.

Moody listened for a while, then got fed up with them. "Let's go back out," he said, "and I'll show you again." And that's exactly what he did. He tore through the front nine in 30. The naysayers were convinced. End of round.

For 27 holes on that remarkable day, Moody shot an amazing 87.

Lowest Nine-Hole Score for a Blindfolded Golfer Using Only a 5-Iron, an 8-Iron, and a Putter

46
Jim England, 1976
Chapparal Country Club
Bullhead City, Arizona

Jim England, of Bullhead City, Arizona, played a round that made him wonder why he ever used a full bag of clubs.

Recalled his wife, Mary, "Fortified with a good supply of confidence-building joy juice, my husband bet some friends he could break 50 on the front side of Chapparal Country Club, using only a 5-iron, 8-iron, and putter. And furthermore, he would hit every shot blindfolded."

So his blindman's bluff was called and he went out to the course with the three clubs and a blindfold. To everyone's amazement, England broke 50 by four strokes, shooting a 46.

The next day, still savoring his victory and counting his modest winnings, he played the front nine again. This time, he had all 14 clubs in his bag and hit all his shots without a blindfold.

He shot a 48!

Most Money Won by a Pro Betting on a Fellow Competitor

$60,000
Bobby Cruickshank, 1930

In 1930, Bobby Jones was the golfing rage of the American sporting public. One of his biggest fans was fellow competitor Bobby Cruickshank.

Like almost every pro golfer, Cruickshank knew that Jones, who maintained his amateur status throughout his playing days, was in a class by himself. Figuring he could never beat Jones, Cruickshank hoped to make money on Jones's victories.

Before the golf season, bookies announced that as great a player as Jones was, they didn't think it was likely that he would win all four majors. Back then, the Grand Slam included the U.S. Open, U.S. Amateur, British Open, and British Amateur. Bookies offered odds of a Jones Grand Slam at 120 to 1.

Cruickshank was so sure Jones would win it all that he wagered $500. Jones proceeded to capture all four majors. While Jones declined to accept any prize winnings, Cruickshank came away with the big bucks, happily pocketing $60,000.

79

Lowest Score Playing St. Andrews by the Light of the Moon

93
Dave Struth, 1876

Well-known Scottish golfer David Struth bet friends that he could play St. Andrews in less than 100 strokes—at night under a full moon.

He beat his goal by seven shots. And, amazingly, he shot his 93 without losing a ball.

Fewest "Strokes" Needed by a Fisherman to Complete a Round

102 "strokes"
J.J. Mackinlay, 1913
Wellington, England

Avid fisherman J.J. Mackinlay scoffed at how difficult golf was while his friend, golfer Rupert May, made light of the skills of anglers. So the two decided to participate in a unique contest.

In a zany handicap match in Wellington, in 1913, Mackinlay used a rod equipped with a 25-ounce weight as his ball and played a round of golf with May, who used his clubs.

Every time Mackinlay cast the weight, it was counted as a "stroke". He consistently cast the weight over 100 yards straight and true on the fairway. But he had trouble trying to hit the cup from short distances.

As a result, Mackinlay lost to May by a score of 87 to 102.

6

Zany
Rules Infractions

Most Penalty Strokes Caused by a Four-Year-Old

4 penalty strokes
Dustin Eggeling
1992 JC Penney Classic

Four-year-old Dustin Eggeling had no idea of the chaos he would cause when he stuffed his own little cut-down 7-iron into the golf bag of his mother, pro golfer Dale Eggeling.

It seemed innocent enough. After all, that's where Mom put her clubs. The problem was that Eggeling didn't know her son's club was in her bag.

She discovered it at the worst possible time—in the middle of a tournament. At the JC Penney Classic in Tarpon Springs, Florida, Eggeling hit a shot on the 15th hole and handed her club to her caddie, who nonchalantly slipped it into the bag. When it wouldn't slide to the bottom, the caddie peered inside and was horrified to see the tiny club jammed in the bottom. Golf rules allow only 14 clubs, and Dustin's 7-iron put Dale over the limit at 15.

A penalty was in order, despite the absurdity of the situation. The rules state that two strokes must be added for every hole the bag is over the limit, with a maximum of four strokes. At the end of the day in the mixed team event, the score of Eggeling and her playing partner, Wayne Levi, zoomed from a 74 to a 78. They finished in 60th place.

"It's apparent that, at some time, Dustin was playing and stuck it in my bag," Eggeling said. "I didn't check. I just screwed up."

A similar incident had happened to Nancy Lopez earlier in the year when she discovered one of her children's toy clubs in her bag during an LPGA tournament. Fortunately for Lopez, she wasn't penalized because the club was plastic and not an official club. Unfortunately for Eggeling, Dustin's cut-down 7-iron fit the definition of a golf club, since it had a definable head and a metal shaft.

Most Severe Penalty Assessed for Being Addicted to Golf

Beheading
Mary, Queen of Scots, 1587

Because of her consuming passion for golf, Mary, Queen of Scots, singlehandedly raised the game's popularity to new heights. Yet, ironically, golf was her downfall and led to her eventual execution.

Scotland—the cradle of golf—actually had banned the sport. In March 1457, King James II decreed "that golf be utterly cryed downe and not used." He was concerned that the Scots, who were constantly battling the English, were devoting too much attention to golf at the expense of archery and, thus, national defense.

A century later, Mary brought golf back into favor in Scotland after she became quite smitten with the game, ironically, in France. When she returned to her homeland after the death of her first husband, Francis, in 1565, the Queen raised plenty of eyebrows. She ignored affairs of state and instead headed out to the links with sons of French nobles serving as her caddies.

Her passion for golf was matched only by her passion for men. After she wed her second husband, Lord Darnley, Mary continued to score on the fairways while her philandering hubby scored in the boudoirs of other women. Because of his constant romantic soirees, Mary found another paramour, who happened to like golf. But a jealous Darnley murdered the Queen's lover.

A short time later, Lord Darnley died in a massive explosion at his home. However, when experts inspected his body, they discovered he had been strangled.

Mary became a suspect, especially when the not-so-grieving widow interrupted her mourning just days after her husband's death to get in a few rounds of golf. Scottish Presbyterians were outraged, and became even more so three months later when Mary wed the Earl of Bothwell. Her shocked subjects felt the Queen had recovered much too quickly from her sorrow.

In 1567 the country's best-known golfer was forced to abdicate her throne. Even worse, she was put on trial for treason in England by Elizabeth I, never known for her fondness for golf. Mary's rounds of golf after Darnley's death were recounted as evidence of her ruthless coldheartedness. She was convicted and then beheaded.

At least Mary made the cut.

Costliest Fine for a Pro Repeating His Favorite Swear Words

$1,000
Ken Green
1991 JC Penney Classic

Pro Ken Green, known for having an extremely colorful vocabulary, discovered it doesn't pay to talk dirty even in jest. In fact, it can be downright costly.

In 1991, Green was playing in the JC Penney

Classic, a mixed team event, with LPGA pro Barb Bunkowsky. In the interview room at Innisbrook Resort in Tarpon Springs, Florida, Green was in a joking mood and talked to reporters about Bunkowsky, who refuses to utter four-letter words. "Being a Christian, she doesn't swear, so I get to swear twice as much—after my shots and hers," Green joked with reporters.

Green explained then that his two favorite epithets on the course were "shit" and "fuck," and then, to underscore his feelings about those words, he repeated them several times.

Once was too many for Connie Wilson of the LPGA media staff. She reported Green's dissertation on obscenities to the PGA Tour office. After a quick investigation, Green was slapped with a $1,000 fine.

"I was kidding around and explaining my theories on those two words," Green said later. "The fine did surprise me. I can understand if I get caught saying it on the golf course and it comes over the tube. Maybe it's a bad habit.

"But there are a lot of bad habits. Smoking is a bad habit, but we're allowed to smoke. Smoking will kill you. Swearing can't."

Biggest Fine for Embarrassing the Tournament Hosts

$475
Mark James
1978 French Open

English pro Mark James thought he'd have a little fun at the final ceremonies of the French Open. With the gallery looking on, officials handed out pay envelopes to the top finishers.

James, who had finished fifth at the European Tour event and won $3,230, opened his envelope with a flourish, then feigned shock when he saw nothing was inside. He showed the empty envelope to the spectators, who laughed heartily.

Tournament officials, however, failed to see the humor. James was fined $475 for "behavior in poor taste."

Explained Ken Schofield, who at the time was secretary of the European Tour, "Everybody on the Tour knows it is the custom to pay the money in sterling the following day." The passing out of pay envelopes to the golfers was for the benefit of the gallery, who weren't supposed to know the envelopes were empty. "That fact was well known to James," added Schofield.

That wasn't the only time James was fined by the Tour. He was assessed a $100 fine for throwing his putter into a tree. "My putter wasn't working and I had had enough of it," James explained. "So I threw it away. I aimed at a lake but it hit the tree."

Most Penalty Strokes for Playing Too Fast

2 penalty strokes
Donnie Hammond
1983 Bay Hill Classic

Donnie Hammond learned the hard way how costly it is to play too fast.

Hammond was playing in his first Bay Hill Classic, in a star-studded pairing that included Jack Nicklaus and David Graham. At the nine-hole turn, Nicklaus ducked into the locker room to relieve himself while Hammond and Graham proceeded onto the 10th tee.

Hammond had shot the front side in only 32 strokes and wasn't anxious to break his rhythm with a lengthy delay. It was Nicklaus's honor on the tee, but the Golden Bear was nowhere in sight.

"After waiting a few minutes, David told me to go ahead and hit so we could get moving," Hammond recalled. "So I did with a drive right in the middle of the fairway. Then he hit, too. We started walking down the fairway when Jack finally showed up."

Nicklaus hit his drive and caught up with Hammond, who wasn't yet an official member of the PGA Tour. Hammond knew something was wrong when Nicklaus put his arm around him. "He told me, 'Donnie, I think we've got a problem,' " Hammond related. " 'I think you're going to have to add two strokes to your score. I'm afraid the rules say we had to play in order.' "

Sure enough, Hammond was assessed the strokes at the end of the round. Graham, though, was spared any penalty because the rule at the time only penalized the first person to hit out of turn. It wouldn't have been a penalty had Hammond hit out of turn by mistake. But because he did it deliberately, he was penalized.

The infraction didn't much matter to Hammond. He shot a horrendous 48 on the back nine and finished in a tie for 40th place.

Longest March by GIs for Insulting Women Golfers

15 miles
Soldiers of the Second Army, 1955
Memphis Country Club
Memphis, Tennessee

Hundreds of GIs from the Second Army learned a lesson in golf etiquette that they would never forget.

The soldiers were in a 45-vehicle convoy heading to maneuvers at Camp Robinson, Arkansas, when they rolled past the Memphis Country Club and spotted two women golfing on the course. Like typical jerks in the days before sexual harassment was even a term, the GIs let loose with a chorus of lusty catcalls such as: "Yoo hoo!" "Fore—play!" "Keep your head down—in my lap!" After the trucks passed, the soldiers hunkered back down in their seats and forgot about the incident.

But General Ben Lear didn't. General Lear was the commander of the Second Army and, by a stroke of luck, had been playing the course as his troops rode by. He heard every one of their crass shouts at the women.

While the convoy proceeded to its destination, General Lear finished his round. Then he phoned Camp Robinson and ordered the soldiers to return to Memphis immediately.

After the convoy retraced the entire 140-mile route, the soldiers dismounted, stood at attention, and listened to a stern lecture from General Lear on golf course etiquette and respect for women.

Then he ordered the GIs to head back to Camp Robinson. But the general made them march the first

15 miles of the journey—which took them past the country club where they had shouted their sexist yells.

To the soldiers who were forced to walk it, the hike was forever known as the "Yoo-Hoo March."

Costliest Mistake by a Tour Pro Caddying for a Friend

2-stroke penalty
Fred Couples
1988 K Mart Greater Greensboro Open

On the Monday preceding the K Mart Greater Greensboro Open, Fred Couples found himself in town with nothing to do. Then he learned that his friend Tom Patri was scheduled to play in the qualifier for one of the four open spots in the tournament.

So Couples volunteered to carry his pal's bag, and Patri readily accepted the help. All went well until the ninth hole after Patri yanked his drive into the rough. Couples dutifully trudged after the ball and found it in the high grass. He then dropped the bag and watched Patri play the shot to the green.

The two had walked only a few feet when they spotted another ball. Fearing the worst, they looked it over—and sure enough, it was Patri's. Couples had made a caddie's worst error, identifying a lost ball as his player's when it really wasn't.

Patri had to take a two-stroke penalty and replay the shot. As a result, he did not make the field for the tournament, missing out on a chance to win some money.

Worst Score of a Hole Halved by Penalty Strokes

Double bogey
John Flannery and Esteban Toledo
1991 Ben Hogan Reno Open

John Flannery and Esteban Toledo ran afoul of the Rules of Golf, triggering the most bizarre finish in Hogan Tour history.

They were locked in a sudden-death playoff at the Ben Hogan Reno Open at Northgate Country Club. On the third extra hole, Flannery marked his ball on the green before attempting a par putt. He was in Toledo's line, so he moved his mark a putter-head length away. Toledo then missed his par putt.

Moments later, Flannery made his putt for what appeared to be a par and the victory. Toledo's caddie then picked up Toledo's marker, figuring that holing out was useless since the playoff was over.

But wait! Flannery had not replaced his ball at the site of the original mark. He forgot that he had moved out of the way of Toledo's putt. Flannery was slapped with a two-stroke penalty, giving him a double bogey.

But Toledo couldn't be declared the winner because he didn't hole out after his caddie picked up his mark. For not properly finishing the hole, Toledo was penalized one stroke. So he, too, scored a double bogey.

As a result, the hole was halved with double bogeys!

However, Flannery's brain sprain didn't cost him the tourney. On the next hole, he made a penalty-free par for the victory.

Most Spirited Fine for Not Wearing the Club Uniform

Six pints of ale
James Dalrymple, 1776
Leith Golf Club
Scotland

Back in the 18th century, it was a serious matter to play at the Leith Golf Club without wearing the official uniform of a red jacket (with the club's crest), a black tie, a white shirt, and beige knickers.

Lieutenant James Dalrymple would find out just how serious when he repeatedly breached the decorum at the Scottish club by playing without his jacket and tie. The Honourable Company of Edinburgh golfers finally had no choice but to take him to task for his repeated oversights.

The club minutes of November 16, 1776, report that the lieutenant was found guilty of playing five times without the requisite wardrobe. His fine was to pay for six pints of ale, presumably downed by those who sat in judgment.

Costliest Penalty for Moving a Boundary Stake

$81,563
Chip Beck
1992 Greater Greensboro Open

In the third round of the Greater Greensboro Open, Chip Beck yanked his tee shot on the 15th hole and watched helplessly as it landed next to an out-of-bounds marker.

When Beck, who was tied for the lead at the time, lined up his next shot, he pulled the stake out of the ground. As he stood there with the marker in his hand, he realized that he might be violating a rule. So he stuck it back into its original position and played the shot.

Alas, it was too late. The act of simply removing the boundary stake, even though he replaced it before hitting his shot, constituted a two-stroke penalty. Those two extra strokes gave him a triple bogey for the hole.

How costly was the infraction? Beck finished in a tie for third in the tournament and earned $53,437. Had he not fiddled with the boundary stake, he would have finished all alone in second place. That would have given him a check for $135,000—a difference of $81,563.

Stiffest Penalty for a Tour Pro Winning a Dinner Bet

One year's probation
Al Besselink
1965 San Diego Open

Al Besselink was a loosey-goosey kind of pro who loved a good wager—even during a PGA event.

Chatting with a friend moments before the first round of the San Diego Open, Besselink told him, "I'll bet you I can break 67 today."

"You're on," said the friend. "Loser buys dinner."

"Nah," retorted Besselink. "Let's really stack the odds in your favor. I'll bet you 10 dinners against your one dinner that I can do it."

For a while it looked like Besselink was going to

be springing for plenty of dinner checks. He started out with five consecutive pars. At the sixth hole, though, Besselink finally nailed a birdie and went on a hot streak. By the time he reached the 18th hole, he needed only to make a par to score 66 and win the bet. Besselink did one better by sinking a 20-foot putt for birdie and a score of 65.

The next day the *San Diego Union* carried a light-hearted story about the wager. But PGA tournament director Jim Gaquin didn't find it funny. He slapped Besselink with a one-year probation. "Besselink lives in one world, we live in another," Gaquin told the press. "We can't allow gambling during regular competition. We'll never try to control $5 Nassaus during practice rounds, but the PGA must retain dignity and respect in the public's eye. Many of the players were upset when Al's gambling hit the press."

Besselink had his own version of why some of his fellow golfers were angry at him. "They didn't like it because I blabbed to the press," he said. "I'm in the limelight, that's all. I guess they thought they had to do something."

Largest Fine in LPGA History

$3,500
Lori Garbacz
1985 LPGA National Pro-Am

Lori Garbacz, one of the most emotional players on the LPGA Tour, holds the record for the stiffest fine ever given a lady pro. At the 1985 LPGA National Pro-Am, she let loose with an obscenity-spiced outburst that was broadcast live on television.

It happened during the third round of the tournament at Denver when Garbacz was protecting her shrinking lead. She had just bogeyed the 15th hole and double-bogeyed the 16th.

A cameraman from ESPN, which was televising the tournament, followed the golfer from the green to the next tee. As Garbacz stood waiting to hit her drive on the 17th, the cameraman continued to crowd her, waiting to get a reaction shot.

Suddenly Garbacz turned and gave him a reaction he'll never forget. "Get that fucking thing out of my face! Do you hear me?" she hollered in exasperation. Every word of her outburst was heard by the nationwide TV audience.

Although she later apologized to golf fans and her fellow pros for "unprofessional behavior," Garbacz was fined a record $3,500 by the LPGA.

Garbacz later explained that she didn't realize the microphone was on and called the tantrum "inadvertent." She added, however, that "it wasn't all my fault. He [the cameraman] should have known better than that. Sometimes I think TV has gone too far with the hand-held camera invading your privacy. I didn't ask him to come there and stick it in my face after a double bogey. I wanted to be myself and get my stuff together for the last two holes."

Largest Fine for Throwing a Ball Out of a Bunker

$500
Dave Hill
1971 Colonial Invitational

Dave Hill, one of the most temperamental golfers in Tour history, was having a rough day at the Colonial

Invitational in Fort Worth, Texas. His shots were going everywhere but where he wanted them to go.

On the 12th hole, his ball landed in yet another bunker. A steaming-mad Hill tromped into the bunker, gave his ball a sneer, then stunned everyone when he bent over and picked it up. The gallery was even more shocked when he tossed the ball like a hook shot in basketball toward the hole.

A thoroughly confused woman scorer, bumbling in awkwardness at the incident, asked Hill what score she should give him for the hole. "Just give me a two," Hill replied, "although I didn't make the basket."

The scorer did as Hill said, realizing that the golfer's round had now become a farce. At the end of the day, Hill compounded the folly by signing his obviously incorrect scorecard. As a result, Hill was summarily disqualified. The disqualification didn't bother him at all because he was playing poorly and wanted out of the event anyway.

In the locker room, Hill told reporters, "I always wanted to try throwing the ball at a hole. I thought I'd give it a try at the Colonial." PGA officials weren't amused and fined Hill $500 for conduct unbecoming a pro.

Biggest Penalty for Playing in a Tournament Without Permission

$500 fine, suspension from the PGA Tour, and removal from the Ryder Cup team
Sam Snead, 1961

A round of golf cost Sam Snead dearly.

After being chosen for the Ryder Cup team for

the 10th time, Snead was fitted for the team uniform and given a travel itinerary to Royal Lytham and St. Anne's in England for the matches.

Because he had played a busy schedule, Snead decided to take some time off before heading overseas. So he wrote to officials of the Portland Open, where he had committed to play, and informed them he wouldn't be participating. That same week, however, he suddenly decided to play in a pro-am in Cincinnati.

He was about to tee off in the event when he learned he might be in violation of a PGA rule. The tour prohibited pros from playing in an event at the same time a sanctioned tournament was in progress. Snead would have to get special permission to play in Cincinnati.

So Sam sent a telegram seeking an official release from his Portland obligation, then played his round. When he finished, he was chagrined to hear the return message from the PGA—permission had been denied.

Realizing he had broken the rule, Snead immediately withdrew from the Cincinnati event, hoping the PGA board would be sympathetic. The officials were not impressed, slapping him with a stiff penalty: a $500 fine and suspension from the PGA Tour for six months. Unfortunately, the dates of the Ryder Cup fell during that six-month period.

Snead filed an appeal, but it was not heard by the PGA until after the Ryder Cup. Thus, he couldn't play in the international event. However, Snead did win a minor victory. His suspension was reduced from six months to 45 days.

The U.S. Ryder Cup team got by nicely without him. With Arnold Palmer playing for the first time, the Americans won by a score of 14½ to 9½.

Most Expensive Shorts Worn by a Pro at a Tournament

$500 shorts
Mark Wiebe
1992 Anheuser-Busch Classic

The PGA Tour has a long-standing prohibition against wearing shorts in an official event, reasoning that regulation long pants preserve golf's status as a true "gentleman's game." And despite the efforts of such notables as Jack Nicklaus to modify the rule, PGA officials have stood firm.

When the temperature reached 102°F at the 1992 Anheuser-Busch Classic at Kingsmill Golf Club in Williamsburg, Virginia, Tour pro Mark Wiebe thought it was too hot to wear long pants. Rule or no rule, he decided comfort was more important than tradition. So he donned some shorts and went to the practice tee.

For giving the rule such short shrift, Wiebe was fined $500.

7

Crazy Equipment
Records

Longest Time a Pro Carried an Out-of-Bounds Stake on Tour

6 months
Roger Maltbie, 1976

Roger Maltbie carried a wooden stake with him on the Tour for six months—not as a weapon against vampires but as a testament to Divine Providence.

Maltbie kept the old, white out-of-bounds marker in his bag because it was an ever-present reminder of a lucky shot that had helped him win the 1976 Memorial Tournament at Muirfield Village in Dublin, Ohio.

Maltbie and Hale Irwin were tied after the regulation 72 holes. During their playoff, Maltbie whacked a tee shot that was headed off the course until, in a remarkable stroke of good fortune, it plunked into the out-of-bounds stake. The ball caromed back toward the fairway, staying in fair territory. Maltbie parred the hole and went on to beat Irwin on the fourth playoff hole.

Overjoyed by his lucky victory, Maltbie pulled up the stake and triumphantly carried it out of Muirfield with him. "I never would have won if it hadn't been for the placement of that stake," Maltbie admitted. "This is my lucky charm." For the remainder of the year, he carried it with him on his stops around the Tour. One day, after a particularly poor performance on the links, he left the stake under his bed in a motel room.

Longest Time Stuck Up a Tree While Trying to Recover a Club

45 minutes
Bobby Knight, 1982
Indiana University Golf Course
Bloomington, Indiana

Indiana University's Bobby Knight plays golf the way he coaches basketball—hurling angry Anglo-Saxon curses as well as anything he can get his hands on. Because of his volatile temper, he has occasionally stormed off the links—and once was stuck up a tree.

One day, while playing on the school's course, Knight missed an easy, short putt on the fifth hole. The putter, being the only thing in his hand, was in trouble. "I tossed it in the air and it hung up in a tree," he confessed to *Golf* magazine years later.

He flung his club so high that it disappeared in a fully grown maple, which promptly gobbled up the putter and refused to drop it. So Knight went stalking off to the next hole.

The following day, Knight had forgiven the offending club. "I wanted it back," he said. "So I went out there by myself and climbed the tree."

First, though, he made sure no one saw him by hustling to the fifth green early in the morning before any golfers had reached the fifth tee. Lifting himself up from branch to branch, Knight found himself 40 feet off the ground, but he still couldn't reach his putter. The coach was experiencing mixed emotions—impressed that he could toss a putter that high up into a tree and peeved that he couldn't retrieve it.

Rather than risk serious injury by going any higher, Knight decided that the putter wasn't all that good anyway and probably would have caused him nothing but more anguish. He was all set to ease his way down the tree when he encountered a new problem.

Golfers had already reached the fifth hole. As a well-known figure on the Indiana campus, Knight couldn't just plop down from a tree. The golfers would instantly recognize him and confirm the assumption that so many already have of the coach—that he's not playing with all his clubs.

So, crouched quietly on a branch high in the maple tree, Knight waited for the group to hole out. But then moments later, another foursome landed their approach shots. So Knight had to remain up in the tree. In fact, he was stuck up there for 45 minutes. Recalled the coach, "I had to wait for four groups to play through before I could come down."

Most Golf Shoes Stolen by a Dog

2 golf shoes
Black Labrador, 1984
Brightondale Park Golf Course
Kansasville, Wisconsin

Before heading onto the links at the Brightondale Park Golf Course, Tom Noonan of nearby Lake Geneva left his golf shoes and bag outside the clubhouse for a few minutes. But when he returned, his shoes were missing.

After asking fellow golfers if they had seen who had swiped his shoes, Noonan found a witness who claimed the culprit was a black Labrador. The dog had picked up one of the shoes, carried it off into the nearby woods, and then come back for the other. A search of the area failed to turn up the shoes or the dog.

"I'd worn those shoes only three times," lamented Noonan. "They cost me sixty bucks—and I'll bet that dog never wore them."

Most Rounds a Pro Played with the Same Ball

4 rounds
Sam Snead
1945 Los Angeles Open

Sam Snead had long held the reputation as one of golf's tightwads, but he outdid himself at the 1945 Los Angeles Open. In an era when golf balls weren't nearly as durable as they are now, Snead played the entire tournament with just one ball!

Actually, he didn't have much choice. It was wartime, there was a national rubber shortage, and golf balls had become very expensive, even for the big spenders who had much looser purse strings than Snead.

"You couldn't get balls then," Snead explained later. "I was paying $100 a dozen. Bing Crosby gave me a ball, a Spalding Dot, and I played it throughout the tournament. The cover was loose, but it kept going."

Incredibly, the ball held up long enough for Slammin' Sam to win the tournament!

Most Consecutive Times Bouncing a Ball on the Head of a Club

3,699 consecutive times
Rob MacGregor, 1990
Blenheim Community Golf Club
Ontario, Canada

Have you ever tried bouncing a golf ball on the face of a sand wedge to see how many times you can do it without messing up?

It's not easy.

In 1990, Rob MacGregor, head professional at the Blenheim Community Golf Club in Ontario, Canada, bounced a ball on the face of his left-handed wedge an incredible 3,699 consecutive times before the ball fell off.

He blew away the previous record set back in 1985 when Mark Mooney, of Hummelstown, Pennsylvania, wore out the face of his pitching wedge by bouncing a ball on it 1,764 times.

Most New Practice Balls Stolen by Golfers in a Tournament

1,008 new practice balls
1991 British Amateur

Golf is a gentleman's game, right?

Try telling that to the Royal and Ancient, the governing body of golf in Europe. The R&A discovered that golf can be a game of light-fingered players.

The R&A, trying to do something a little special for competitors at the 1991 British Amateur, provided 84 dozen just-out-of-the-box bright and shiny balata balls for the practice range. The R&A shelled out $44 a dozen, or $3,696 for 1,008 balata balls.

Apparently, the temptation by the tourney participants to swipe the balls was just too great. By the end of the British Amateur, all the balatas were gone—carried off by golfers who felt these balls were too good to be used on the practice range.

Most Heroic 2-Iron Shot Ever Made

Larry LeBoeuf, 1992
Ptarmigan Country Club
Fort Collins, Colorado

Larry LeBoeuf's best 2-iron shot ever had nothing to do with the ball he hit, but rather the club he *threw*.

While approaching the sixth hole at Ptarmigan Country Club, LeBoeuf and his pals saw an automobile pull up beside the green and a teenager hop out. While the golfers watched in disbelief, the teen grabbed the flagstick from the hole and then bolted back into the car, which squealed off at high speed.

Knowing the road doubled back alongside the seventh fairway, LeBoeuf yanked his 2-iron from his golf bag and dashed off in hot pursuit. He raced across the fairway, but getting to the road was another story. He had to plod through an eight-foot-wide creek, climb up an embankment, and then scramble through a barbed wire fence.

Just as LeBoeuf reached the road, he saw the car barreling toward him. With all the skill of an Australian boomerang tosser, LeBoeuf hurled his 2-iron at the car. His timing was perfect. The club ricocheted off the open passenger-side window and, incredibly, smacked into the flagstick, knocking it from the hands of the young thief. LeBoeuf then triumphantly retrieved the stolen pin and his trusty 2-iron.

It was no big deal, LeBoeuf told those who congratulated him. With tongue firmly planted in cheek, he said, "When you've had as much practice as I have in hitting the flagstick with a 2-iron, this isn't all that spectacular."

Highest Rate of Inflation of the Price of a Putter

$60 in four hours
Purchased by Gary Player, 1961
Tokyo, Japan

Gary Player and Arnold Palmer were in Tokyo in 1961 for the opening of a new golf course. The greens were slow, so Player went browsing in the pro shop for a putter that he thought would punch the ball a bit more briskly across the higher grass.

In a barrel of putters, Player found an elongated black blade that seemed just what he was looking for. It had enough loft, Player reasoned, to make the ball roll better on the slow greens. Best of all, it had a price tag that was the equivalent of only $5.

Player held the putter up for Palmer's approval. But Arnie shook his head and suggested that Player continue searching for a better putter.

So Player left the shop empty-handed. But he couldn't get his mind off the putter. So after playing a round with Palmer, he walked back into the shop to buy it.

Player was shocked to see a new price tag on the putter. A shop attendant had noticed the golfer's earlier interest in the club and decided that if it was that good a putter, then $5 was probably way too little to charge for it. Now, the putter had a new tag—$65.

Player protested over the price, but to no avail. Reluctantly, he paid the inflated cost.

Today, Player considers the $65 a bargain. He since has used the putter to win dozens of tournaments around the world, earning him millions of dollars.

Most Consecutive Rounds Played with the Same Ball

46 consecutive rounds
Judge Michael Nehemiah Manning, 1928–29
Taladega, Alabama

Judge Michael Nehemiah Manning didn't have to budget much money each year for golf balls.

Judge Manning purchased a Kro-Flite golf ball on November 15, 1928, and retired it on January 28, 1929, after using it to play 46 rounds of 18 holes each. His average score per round was 82, which means he whacked the ball approximately 2,000 times, exclusive of putts.

Whenever the ball sailed off the fairway, the judge pursued it with vigor. He and his playing partners would search among the weeds, many times taking more than the allotted five minutes to look for it.

Obviously, they don't make players—or golf balls—like they used to.

Most Expensive Set of Clubs Made from a Ship's Propeller

$16,500
From the Queen Elizabeth 2

Probably never in history have golf clubs been made from such an unlikely metal source. But when the world's last great Cunard ocean liner, the *Queen Elizabeth 2*, was refitted in 1986–87, its two original propellers were replaced.

Each propeller contained a massive amount of rare metal—32½ tons of a marine bronze alloy called Superston 70. The alloy offered both strength and the color of platinum, with a nice tinge of gold. The active minds at Sandhill Limited, a Yorkshire, England, precious metals company, proposed a great moneymaking idea. Why not melt the propellers down and turn them into golf clubs?

So the metal from the melted-down props was sent to the Swilken clubmakers at St. Andrews, Scotland. (Appropriately, the *Queen Elizabeth 2* was originally built and outfitted in Scotland.) Swilken craftspeople then fashioned the metal into golf sets, each priced at a whopping $16,500. Each set included three persimmon woods (1-3-5), 10 irons (1-SW), and a putter. That comes to $1,178.57 per club.

There were other goodies thrown in with the set—a leather bag, an umbrella, a shirt, a dozen balls, a towel, shoe bags, a ball marker, and even tees. Everything, incidentally, sported the *QE2* logo.

Most Lost Balls Found by a Pro Without Finding His Own

26 balls
Mark Brooks
1991 Las Vegas Invitational

Mark Brooks had some bad news, good news, and even more bad news during the Las Vegas Invitational.

The bad news was that he lost two balls. The good news was that he found 26 balls while looking for his lost ones. But the more bad news was that none of them were his!

After battling near the lead with excellent scores of 67 and 65, Brooks hit into trouble in the third round on the 17th hole when an errant shot lodged high in a palm tree.

A cherry picker was summoned to hoist Brooks up into the tree so he could try to locate his ball. He poked around through the fronds and gathered eight balls. But none were his, so he was forced to take a stroke-and-distance penalty. It cost him a double bogey and he finished the round with a 74.

The next day, Brooks suffered further misfortune, this time at the 18th hole. After placing his approach shot safely on the green, he marked his ball, picked it up, and tossed it to his caddie. But his caddie missed the ball. To their horror, the ball rolled into a greenside lake before it could be stopped.

The rules say a player will be penalized two strokes if he doesn't complete the hole with the same ball that he played off the tee. So Brooks took off his shoes and socks, rolled up his pants, and waded into the water. He fished around with his hands and his feet, eventually pulling up 18 balls. Alas, none were his. So once again he had to take two penalty strokes for a double bogey, giving him a 78 for the day.

For the tournament, Brooks found a total of 26 balls, all belonging to other unlucky golfers—but none as unlucky as he was.

Most Kids Scrambling to Swipe Tees at a Golfing Event

50 kids (estimated)
Walter Hagen and Joe Kirkwood exhibition,
1922
Shennecosset Club
Groton, Connecticut

Curiously enough, it wasn't the mere presence of the famed Walter Hagen and Australian traveling mate Joe Kirkwood that persuaded officials to rope off the crowds. What got out of hand was the uncontrollable scramble for the golfers' tees.

Hagen and Kirkwood were among the first pros ever to use wooden tees, which had just been invented. The golfers introduced them during an exhibition at the Shennecosset Club.

"Joe and I strutted around the course with the bright red tees stuck behind our ears," Hagen recalled. "At each tee we used them and left them. Kids scrambled onto the course, grabbing them as souvenirs. They became so popular that the club found it necessary to rope off the tees and fairways to control the galleries. This was the first time in U.S. golf history that gallery-control ropes were used."

The wooden tees revolutionized golf. For centuries, players hit their drives off earth-made tees fashioned from a handful of dirt. In 1921, Dr. William Lowell, a dentist from Maplewood, New Jersey, grew tired of coming home from a round of golf with dirty hands and clothes. So he whittled little pegs from a wooden flagpole in front of his home. Then he began mass-producing his tees, which he painted red and called Reddy Tees.

In 1922, he gave them to Hagen and Kirkwood to promote on their exhibition tour. By 1926 there were more than 200 different brands of tees marketed by competitors.

Smallest Club Ever Used by a Professional Golfer

18 inches
Joe Kirkwood

Australian trick-shot artist Joe Kirkwood swung the world's tiniest golf club—a wedge that was only 18 inches long! Time and again, he could chip the ball onto the green from 50 yards out with the little wedge.

Longest Club Ever Used by a Professional Golfer

10 feet
Joe Kirkwood

Joe Kirkwood not only could hit with a tiny club, he also could wield a big stick.

During the height of his career, the legendary Aussie trickster often would tee off with a driver that was a whopping ten feet long.

Highest Percentage of Holes in One Made with One Club

1.000
Rick Pierce, 1992
Orlando, Florida

Rick Pierce, a time-share salesman from Orlando, has a 6-iron hanging over the mantel of his home because the club has achieved perfection. The first and only time Pierce ever swung it, he knocked the ball into the 15th hole at MetroWest Country Club for an ace.

He never swung the club again.

Pierce had bought the club—a Tommy Armour 845 6-iron—as part of a replacement set after some-one broke into his pickup truck and swiped all his clubs. Though he had been an avid, near-scratch golfer, Pierce was so upset that he didn't bother buy-ing the new set for five months.

"Finally, one day, the guys I worked with pes-tered me into buying some clubs and then we headed right out to MetroWest to play," Pierce recalled. "We got to the course late so I didn't even have time to hit a practice shot. I was peeling the plastic off the clubs on the first tee."

For someone who hadn't touched a club in five months since the burglary, Pierce was playing well. After 14 holes, he was only five over par, already up "$30 or $40" on the friends who had goaded him into playing.

Then, at the par-3, 168-yard 15th hole, Pierce had

an impending shot that required his 6-iron for the first time. He tore off the plastic, forgetting to remove the adhesive that kept the plastic affixed to the shaft.

"I don't take practice swings, and as I stood over the ball with the club motionless, I noticed the adhesive for the first time," Pierce said. "I thought for a moment about backing away and removing it, but then I thought, 'Nah, just go ahead and hit it.' "

With one swing—his only swing ever with this particular club—Pierce stunned himself and his playing partners by knocking the ball into the cup for an ace. After jumping up and down and giving high-fives to his playing partners, Pierce knew immediately what he would do with his 6-iron.

"I shoved that club right back into the bag and didn't take it out again," he recalled. "After the round, I went to the pro shop and had them order me another 6-iron. This one will never be hit again. It's the perfect club."

Cheapest Ransom Paid to Retrieve a Captive Golf Ball

25-cent can of dog food
Larry Compton, 1969
Seminole Lake Country Club
Largo, Florida

Larry Compton, of Needham, Massachusetts, was playing the 17th hole at Seminole Lake Country Club when his golf ball became involved in a hostage situation.

Compton over-clubbed his tee shot and watched it arch over a fence lining the fairway and into a backyard. When the golfer approached the house, he noticed a very unfriendly dog snarling at him.

Behind the menacing dog was a sign that read, "Your ball will cost you a can of dog food." Compton realized that if he wanted his $1.25 ball back, he would have to pay up. So the next day, on his way to the course, the golfer stopped by a supermarket and picked up a can of dog food for 25 cents. Then he went to the house, asking for his ball. He got it back, after handing over the can to a very enterprising 14-year-old boy.

Most Lost Golf Balls That Fell Out of a Tree at One Time

105 lost golf balls
Olympic Club, 1977
San Francisco, California

A big cypress guarding the eighth green at the Lake-side Course at San Francisco's Olympic Club must have been the most cursed tree on the planet.

In 1977, maintenance men gave three huge branches of the old tree a trimming. The men were stunned when the tree showered them with 105 stray balls that it so unforgivingly had gobbled up.

Most Golf Balls Received by a Baseball Superstar as a Gift

3,000 golf balls
George Brett, 1992
Kansas City Royals

Although Fred Couples is one of the top players in golf today, he loves watching baseball more than his own sport.

His favorite major leaguer is his close friend, George Brett, retired superstar of the Kansas City Royals, who owns a home in Couples's neighborhood in Palm Springs, California. The two often played golf together in the off-season.

When Brett collected his milestone 3,000th hit in 1992, Couples wanted to present his pal with a unique gift. So the golfer boxed up 3,000 Slazenger golf balls and sent them to his baseball buddy, assuming that Brett wouldn't have to buy another ball for the rest of his life.

"His garage should be full," Couples said.

8

Weird Course
Records

Most Hazards That Moo on a Golf Course

80 hazards that moo
Dannebrog Golf Club
Dannebrog, Nebraska

Playing golf at the Dannebrog Golf Club is a mooing experience.

Although there are no sand traps or trees, Dannebrog features sand greens and some beefy hazards—cows. More than 80 bovines are free to graze the fairways and rough of the par-34, nine-hole, 2,620-yard course.

"You have to look out for the cow pies," said Ed Boltz, secretary-treasurer of the golf club. "If your ball lands in one, you're allowed a free drop.

"If the cow is on the fairway, you just have to learn to shoot over him or under him. It's not too often that a ball actually hits a cow.

"Every once in a while, a cow might try to eat a ball. If it does happen, then the golfer gets to hit the ball over again with no penalty. Sometimes, a golfer will find slobber all over his ball because a cow picked it up and spit it out."

Golfers are willing to put up with the cows because the animals keep maintenance costs down by helping fertilize the fairways and "mowing" the grass. Greens fees are only $2 and an annual membership is just $15 ($20 for a family).

The cows come into play because the links are part of pasture land that is leased to the golf club by a farmer for $2.50 a year on the condition that the bovines are free to roam the course. (Wire fences keep them off the sand greens.)

A Winged Foot or Pebble Beach it ain't. But the club does boast more than 90 members and hosts an annual tournament in August, called the Bull Pen

Open, which draws over 150 participants from all over the country every year.

The 380 residents of Dannebrog hope the event will grow into a major tournament. But that kind of thinking is probably just cow pie in the sky.

Most Golfers Arrested by Their Playing Partner

3 golfers
New York State Trooper Stan Garrant, 1992
McCann Memorial Golf Course
Poughkeepsie, New York

State Trooper Stan Garrant, a self-proclaimed golfaholic, had just finished his shift and stopped by McCann Memorial Golf Course to get in a quick 18 holes before heading home. At the pro shop, he was directed to join a threesome already on the first tee.

As he approached, Garrant observed some very suspicious activity. One of the men lighted a cigarette, then passed it around to the others, who each proceeded to puff and inhale deeply. The officer knew he was dealing with problem grass—and it wasn't the kind he often encountered in the rough.

Garrant identified himself to the trio as the fourth member of the foursome—and as a law enforcement officer. He then escorted his playing partners into the clubhouse and called the Poughkeepsie police department because the marijuana smoking occurred in its jurisdiction.

With the golfers' arrest, Garrant's anticipated round on the links went up in smoke.

Most Golf Carts Used in Tank Training Exercises on a Golf Course

12 golf carts
Company A, 3rd Battalion,
37th Armor Division, 1988
Custer Hill Golf Course
Fort Riley, Kansas

Golfers didn't know whether to gape in amazement or dive for cover when troops in full combat gear conducted tank training exercises on the fairways and roughs—in golf carts!

In 1988, Major General Leonard Wischart, commander of Fort Riley, was looking for ways to cut training costs on the base. When someone suggested that thousands of dollars could be saved by training potential M1 Abrams tank drivers in golf carts, the commander "tanked him" and ordered it done.

So the 200 troops of Company A, 3rd Battalion, 37th Armor Division headed for Custer Hill—a golf course designed by famed Robert Trent Jones, who never dreamed that his creation would one day be used for tank maneuvers. Neither did the golfers who were on the course playing that day.

The Army paid $289 for rental of a dozen carts and greens fees and then deployed the troops in trees and bushes throughout the course. Bunkers and hazards weren't for playing golf; they were for playing war. Instead of using 32-foot, 60-ton tanks with 105-mm cannons, tank drivers operated four-by-six-foot E-Z-Gos.

"Imagine our surprise when over the rise on a fairway hill we saw golf carts driven by camouflaged soldiers," said golfer Robert Smith. "We were wondering if the golf course was under siege."

Added playing partner Mark Johnson, "We thought we'd help them out by lofting some golf balls in their direction so they could pretend the shots were incoming."

Although the Army took plenty of ribbing for using the golf carts, officials pointed out it would have cost $20,000 more if they had used M1 Abrams. Besides, they added, the drills were useful. Said First Sergeant Leslie Axton, "It's the same as playing in a sandbox with little bitty tanks."

Most Nations Which a Hole Crosses

2 nations
Green Zone Golf Course
Haparanda, Sweden

Golfers can tee off in one country and hole out in another at the Green Zone Golf Course near Haparanda, Sweden.

The 132-yard, par-3 sixth hole straddles the Swedish-Finnish border so that the tee shot is in Sweden and the cup is in Finland. It's the only course with a customs office and a scorecard that includes customs regulations instead of only ground rules. However, passports are not required for playing the course.

It can take over an hour just to make a four-foot putt on the sixth hole because the border that goes across the green divides not only the two countries, but also two time zones.

Because the course is an hour from the Arctic

Circle, the sun doesn't set during the summer. As a result, golfers can play around the clock from June to August.

Most Four-Legged Caddies on One Course

2 four-legged caddies
Talamore Golf Course
Pinehurst, North Carolina

Llamas have llightened the lload of llinksmen at the Talamore Golf Course.

When the club first opened in October 1991, the management decided it would get the edge on its competitors by offering golfers a service found nowhere else. It's the world's only course where a player can hire two four-legged caddies—llamas named Billy and Dollie.

"With 32 golf courses in this area, we wanted to get a little identity that the others wouldn't have," said club pro John McDougald. "We're the only course in the world that has llamas. They make great caddies and they have a payload of 400 pounds, so two 50-pound bags of golf clubs are no big deal."

For $400 ($100 a bag), four golfers can rent the two llamas. The pack animals, purchased from a breeder in Vermont, are equipped with special saddles that allow golfers to walk the course while the four-legged caddies each carry two golf bags. A handler leads the llamas and draws clubs for the players.

When nature calls for Billie and Dollie, they are respectful of the course, taking care to handle their private business in the rough. And they also are respectful of the golfers and their shots.

"They give a little grunt on good shots," McDougald said. "But if it's a bad shot, they don't say a word."

Not only are the furry caddies a first, but so is the course's unique Rule Number 4: "Golf carts yield right of way to llamas."

Longest Average Time to Play an 18th Hole

60 minutes
Mt. Dundas Country Club
Mt. Dundas, Greenland

The 18th hole at Mt. Dundas Country Club takes an average of an hour to play—assuming you have mountain-climbing gear. Otherwise, you can't reach it at all.

The hole sits atop Mt. Dundas, a 720-foot peak in Greenland, 700 miles north of the Arctic Circle and only 800 miles from the North Pole. Nearby is Thule Air Force Base, where every July 4 the U.S. airmen compete in the annual Dundas Open.

Mt. Dundas is a tortuous course where the rough and fairways are strewn with rocks and the "greens" are 10-foot-in-diameter circles filled with sand.

It's a nine-hole, par-36 layout with no sand bunkers or water hazards—just the result of centuries of sliding glaciers. Crevices, knolls, pebbles, and boulders make for imposing obstacles, and the fairways are adjacent to slopes that drop off treacherously, seemingly to nowhere.

In the Dundas Open, each player carries a square

of carpet from which he hits his shots. He completes a hole by stopping his ball on the sand green, which is rimmed by rocks. He has just one golf club and two balls. If he loses both balls in one of the crevices or cliffs, then he's disqualified.

It's golf at its crudest, most elementary state— particularly on the brutal closing hole, which takes about an hour to play.

The approach shot must carry to the top of a plateau. Then, to reach your ball, you must use mountain-climbing gear to scale a difficult 60-degree incline. "In the Dundas Open," said one competitor, "just getting to the green is a major challenge. Golfing is the easy part."

Most Yards That a Green Moves Back and Forth

100 yards
14th green
Coeur d'Alene Resort Golf Course
Coeur d'Alene, Idaho

One of the most amazing greens on earth, the par-3 14th hole at Coeur d'Alene Resort Golf Course is a floating island that can be moved to within 75 yards of the tee or be shoved back as far as 175 yards away.

Course owner Duane Hagadone got the idea for the floating green when he observed a cluster of logs floating in the lake near a sawmill. So he had golf architect Scott Miller design it. A naval engineering firm drew up the blueprints and a shipbuilder constructed the green in sections, assembled it on the lakefront, and towed it into place.

The 15,000-square-foot, state-of-the-art green,

Most Yards a Clubhead Flew off the Shaft

25 yards
Faye Shelbourne, 1988
Victoria, British Columbia

Faye Shelbourne thought it would be quite interesting to use her grandmother's antique clubs during a 1988 round of golf.

It proved to be that—and more. Faye learned the hard way that older doesn't necessarily mean better. As she went into her backswing on the first hole, the club head flew off. To her dismay, the club head soared an estimated 25 yards.

It would have gone further—except it smashed through a window of the pro shop.

9

Outlandish
Putting Records

Most Putts Needed to Hole Out

156 putts
A.J. Lewis, 1890
Peacehaven Golf Course
Sussex, England

Putt is a four-letter word, and for golfers the world over, it can turn into a string of four-letter words. That's because the putt may be the most frustrating shot in all of golf.

English amateur A.J. Lewis found that out for himself.

For sheer putting ineptitude, perhaps no one will ever approach his "feat". Lewis acknowledged he was a bad golfer and then went out and proved it. After taking more than two dozen shots to reach a par-3 hole at the Peacehaven Golf Course, Lewis needed an astounding 156 putts to hole out.

Longest Putt Made by a Grasshopper

¹/₄ inch
Scarborough South Cliff Course, 1921
Yorkshire, England

One of God's little creatures helped out a grateful linksman during a 1921 match at the Scarborough South Cliff Course in Yorkshire.

Paul McGregor needed only to sink a 20-foot putt to win the match. But his heart sank as his putt hung on the lip of the cup and wouldn't fall.

However, just then a grasshopper bounded onto the green and landed on the ball. The insect's motion was just enough to nudge the ball that final ¼ inch as it plopped into the hole, giving McGregor the victory.

Longest Putt Conceded for a "Gimme" in Ryder Cup Competition

4 feet
Jack Nicklaus, 1969
Royal Birkdale Golf Club
Southport, England

In one of the most exciting finishes ever in Ryder Cup competition, it came down to the final putt on the final hole of the final match between Jack Nicklaus and Tony Jacklin.

After Nicklaus made his par putt, Jacklin faced a four-footer that he needed to hole for the British team to salvage a tie. If he missed the pressure putt, the U.S. team would win.

Nicklaus, though, didn't make Jacklin putt it. In a move that stunned fellow teammates and competitors alike, the Golden Bear picked up Jacklin's marker—in effect declaring the putt "good." As a result, the tourney ended in a 16–16 tie, the only deadlock in Ryder Cup history.

Nicklaus was immediately hailed around the world for this extraordinary act of sportsmanship. But not everyone thought it was right. Frank Beard, a member of the American squad, said most of his teammates were upset.

"Oh, we were irate—I was, for sure," Beard wrote in his book *Making the Turn.* "It may have been a great gesture for Jack Nicklaus, but the other eleven of us had worked very hard and we wanted to win. He just arrogantly assumed that the team and the country, individually and together, would want him to make this sporting gesture. . . .

"I've heard people say it was a very short putt, something in the one- or two-foot range. The putt was actually no less than four feet, and my guess at the time was five.

"Looking back, I recognize the conceded putt as the act of a man of considerable class and sophistication. But I guarantee you, if I'd had the same decision to make, Tony Jacklin would have had to show us he could make a four-footer with the weight of a whole nation on his shoulders."

Longest Measured Putt to Save a Quadruple Bogey

127 feet
Floyd Slasor, 1972
Moon Valley Country Club
Phoenix, Arizona

Floyd Slasor, of Phoenix, Arizona, was on Moon Valley's 10th green, 127 feet away from the pin, when he putted the ball firmly in the direction of the flag.

Incredibly, the ball dropped in for what was the longest measured putt at the time. After Slasor finished his round, club members had already heard of the remarkable coast-to-coaster. The golfer politely accepted their congratulations, then felt compelled to make an embarrassing admission.

"It wasn't for a birdie," he told them. "It was for an eight."

Most Consecutive Holes in Which a Golfer Putted One Stroke Less Than the Previous Hole

5 consecutive holes
Willard Moore, 1977
Tides Country Club
St. Petersburg, Florida

Willard Moore of Hopkinsville, Kentucky, was playing the Tides Country Club when he experienced one of the most unusual putting oddities in golf.

Not quite used to the greens when he began his round, Moore four-putted the first hole. He was still struggling on the second green with a three-putt. But he improved on the third hole by two-putting, and he kept alive his streak of putting a stroke better on each successive hole with a one-putt on Number 4.

At the par-3 fifth hole, there was only one thing Moore could possibly do to make one less putt than the previous hole. And that was not to have to putt at all. Incredibly, Moore finished the hole without a putt. After missing the green with his tee shot, he proceeded to chip in on his next swing.

Moore had completed a rare progression of putts—4-3-2-1-0.

Longest Putt Holed After Being Shot with a Pellet Gun

30 feet
Dr. Tom Jones, 1992
New Albany Country Club
New Albany, Indiana

As Dr. Tom Jones was bending over to line up a 30-footer on the 10th green, a shot rang out. Suddenly, the doctor grabbed his rear and yelped in pain.

His posterior, clad in bright red pants, had been too inviting a target for a youngster wielding a pellet gun. The kid and his two accomplices had been lying in ambush on a brush-lined creek bank across from the green, waiting for the right bull's-eye to come along.

Dr. Jones was not a man who stood idly by after his butt had just taken a potshot. He sprinted across the creek, through the thick brush, and collared one of the youngsters. The culprit quickly ratted on the other two and they were all turned over to the New Albany police.

Most golfers would have considered their round finished after such an assault. But not Dr. Jones. He returned to the 10th green, where his partners were still waiting. And so was his 30-footer.

Again, he lined up his putt and, with remarkable nerves and concentration, knocked the ball right into the cup.

Most Putts Stroked with a Worn-Out Hip Joint

2,500 (estimated)
Claude Petrov
St. Louis, Missouri

When amateur Claude Petrov told his fellow golfers that he was the hippest putter around, he meant it.

He played with a unique putter—one made from his worn-out manufactured hip joint.

Shortly after he started playing golf at the age of 65, Petrov needed a hip joint replaced with a synthetic one. But five years later, in 1978, the prosthesis wore out.

This time his doctor decided to replace the man-made joint with a bone graft.

"What are you going to do with the prosthesis?" Claude asked.

"Throw it away," his doctor replied.

"Hold on just a minute," Claude said. "I can do something with it."

The doctor removed the old joint—which included a steel pin 10 inches long—and handed it over to Petrov. While he was recovering, the 70-year-old golfer found someone who could fashion the old joint into a putter.

"Now I'm playing with my new hip, and putting with my old hip—and doing it very well," Petrov reported shortly after the surgery.

Most Time Elapsed Between the Final Two Putts to Win the U.S. Open

12 minutes
Jack Nicklaus
1962 U.S. Open

In all the excitement of winning the 1962 U.S. Open, Jack Nicklaus forgot to hole out.

Nicklaus and Arnold Palmer had been locked in an 18-hole playoff at Oakmont Country Club near Pittsburgh. Palmer, who grew up just 30 miles away in Latrobe, did not have a good day. On the 18th green, he holed out with a 74, three strokes behind Nicklaus, whose ball was just 30 inches from the cup. Realizing victory was virtually impossible, Palmer walked over to Nicklaus' ball and, being the gracious man that he is, picked it up and handed it to Nicklaus, conceding the putt, and, thus, the match.

The gallery raced onto the green, engulfing the two players and caddies, along with the marshals and scorers. Nicklaus and Palmer were being swept toward the scorer's tent when an alert United States Golf Association official noted there was a rules oversight.

In medal play, which the Open is, an opponent cannot concede a putt. Each stroke must be made over the entire 18 holes. Had Nicklaus signed his scorecard with a score of 71, he would have been disqualified for signing an incorrect total.

Joe Dey, the secretary of the USGA, received the news in stunned disbelief, then realized that an error had indeed been committed. He was able to reach Nicklaus before the winner had signed his scorecard and ushered him to the green so the final stroke could be made.

After a lengthy delay, Dey placed Nicklaus's ball at a spot thought to be where Palmer had picked it up. Nicklaus then crouched over the ball, studied the line momentarily, and drained the putt to officially seal his victory.

Most Strokes Needed by a Pro Putting from Three Feet Away

12 strokes
Brian Barnes
1968 French Open
St. Cloud, France

Brian Barnes, a British Ryder Cup player, was among the leaders in the second round of the 1968 French Open. But he lost his composure completely on the short par-3 eighth hole.

Putting for a bogey four from three feet away, Barnes tried to rake the ball into the hole like an irate Monte Carlo croupier at the craps table. But it was no dice holing out.

Fuming mad, Barnes turned his putter into a hockey stick and batted the ball back and forth—while it was still moving. But he still couldn't knock it in the cup.

Too infuriated to worry about penalty strokes, Barnes acted as if the ball were a mouse and his club a broom. He swatted at the ball while he hopped around the green. The ball still dodged the hole. In total frustration, Barnes even played a stroke croquet style—by standing astride the line of the putt—in another violation of the rules. This exercise in masochism took all of 30 seconds before finally the ball plopped into the cup.

His astonished playing partner had tried frantically to keep score, but wasn't sure of the count, what with all the penalty strokes and all. With total disregard for his own safety, the marker asked the seething Barnes, "Well, when you catch your ass in a buzz saw, it's not too easy to tell how many teeth bit you. What did you make?"

Displaying the only self control he had shown throughout his débâcle, Barnes refrained from lunging at his playing partner's throat. Instead he bellowed, "Twelve!" But that was only for his disastrous play on the green. Barnes actually shot a 15 for the hole.

Barnes was through counting. In fact, he was through with the tournament, and stalked off the course, still raging mad.

10

Silly Mishaps

First British Soldier Killed by a Golf Ball

Private David Barnet, 1914
Wormit Golf Course
Fifeshire, Scotland

The most astonishing and tragic death from a golf ball occurred in the summer of 1914 at Wormit Golf Course in Fifeshire.

The soldier, Private David Barnet, was with the Fourth Black Watch, which was training for future duty in France to fight in World War I. In fact, they were only days away from being shipped to the Continent. Barnet's group was going through manoeuvers in a field adjacent to the golf course where a women's tournament was underway.

During the competition, one of the contestants pulled her tee shot. Her errant ball sailed off the course and struck Barnet in the temple. The soldier, who wasn't wearing his helmet at the time, collapsed on the spot. He was rushed to the hospital where he died two days later.

Barnet's death was by no means the only fatal accident to happen on a golf course. Numerous other deaths have been recorded on the links.

One of the most freaky occurred in 1963. Harold Kalles, of Toronto, Canada, was mortally wounded when his throat was cut by a golf club shaft that broke against a tree as he was trying to play out of a bunker.

Longest Drive Ever to Strike a Spectator

506 yards
George Bayer, 1948
Las Vegas, Nevada

George Bayer stood 6'5½" tall and was known as one of the longest hitters ever on the PGA Tour.

Playing in a tournament in Las Vegas, Bayer hit a drive that rocketed off the tee. Fans whistled in awe as the ball flew over 400 yards on the fly. The ball bounced once on the green and then plunked a stunned spectator on the shoulder. The gallery was even more impressed because Bayer's long-distance drive hit a fan who was standing about 30 yards behind the flagstick—of a 476-yard hole!

That wasn't the longest shot of Bayer's career, though. Once, playing in Sydney, Australia, Bayer's shot on a 586-yard par-5 was so close to the green that he needed only a short chip to reach it. Ever the modest one, he noted, "I had a following wind."

Fewest Seconds After Hitting the Ball Before Getting Knocked Out by One's Own Shot

3 seconds
B.D. Wakasugi, 1923
Chislehurst, England

In 1923, B.D. Wakasugi, secretary at the Japanese Embassy in London, decided to play golf at Chislehurst, a wonderful old course designed by the great Willie Park, Jr.

Wakasugi teed up his ball on the fourth hole and whacked it with all his might. The ball slammed directly into a post about 10 yards from the tee. Then the ball flew straight back—and crashed into the golfer's forehead. The impact knocked Wakasugi unconscious.

Most Cows Killed by a Tee Shot

1 cow
W.J. Robinson, 1934
Kent Golf Course
England

On the 18th hole of a 1934 match at a golf course in Kent, English pro W.J. Robinson was gunning for a birdie. He scored a cow instead.

Back then, cows were allowed to graze in the rough.

Robinson launched a tee shot that soared off the fairway and struck a grazing cow square on the back of the head, killing the animal instantly.

Most Holes Played While Holding an Ice Bag to One's Head

11 holes
Greg Powers
1982 Greater Erie Charity Classic

Aside from the usual number of clubs in his bag, golfer Greg Powers needed one piece of extra equipment to complete a tournament—an ice bag.

For 11 holes, at the 1982 Greater Erie (Pennsylvania) Charity Classic, Powers walked down the fairway holding an ice bag to the left side of his forehead after knocking himself out in a freak accident.

On the eighth hole of the final round, Powers uncorked a wild tee shot that finally settled behind a tree. Surveying the awkward situation, Powers realized he had virtually no room to follow through on his swing.

One option was to accept his fate and move the ball a club length away, declaring it an unplayable lie with the resulting one-stroke penalty. However, since he did have room for a backswing, Powers decided to go through with the shot, knowing that his club would stop abruptly as soon as he made contact with the ball.

He selected a 3-iron and took a full swing. The ball sailed off, but his club whacked into the tree. The shaft snapped on impact and the clubhead whipped all the way around the trunk, smacking Powers on the left side of the forehead. The blow left the golfer sprawled unconscious on the ground for five minutes. Doctors were summoned and, after an on-site examination, advised him to withdraw from the tournament.

But the plucky Powers refused, reasoning his only injury was a bad headache and some bruised pride. After a marshal gave him an ice bag to help hold down the swelling and to numb the area, Powers continued to play. For the rest of the round, he held the ice bag to his temple until it was time for him to hit. Then he put it down, took the shot, and immediately placed the ice bag back on the injured area.

Ironically, Powers actually played better with the ice bag than he had prior to the mishap. He shot the final 11 holes in three under par, finishing the day with a 65, and a total of 134 for the two-day tournament.

That was good enough for fourth place, but Powers wasn't around to accept any congratulations. As soon as he signed his scorecard after the 18th hole, he was taken to Erie Hospital. There, an examination determined he had suffered a concussion.

Longest Time a Pro Was Locked Out of His Hotel Room in the Nude

45 minutes
Sam Torrance, 1991
Nice, France

Following a round at the 1991 Mediterranean Open in Nice, France, Scottish pro Sam Torrance returned to his hotel late in the afternoon, doffed all his clothes, and lounged outside on the balcony of his room.

143

What started out as a relaxing respite turned into an embarrassing predicament.

Stretched out in the nude, Torrance let the ocean breezes flow over his body. He was drifting off to sleep when suddenly a gust of wind slammed the door shut. Torrance got up and, with a sickening feeling in his stomach, reached for the handle. As he feared, the door was locked.

For a full 45 minutes, as the sun set and a cool, damp breeze swept in off the ocean, Torrance stood shivering in the buff. He was finally rescued after he hailed a shocked passerby below, told him his tale of woe, and asked him to send up help.

The next day, Torrance exposed himself to further mortification when he shot a pitiful 77.

Most Major Ailments in a
Professional Career

9 major ailments
Andy North, 1970–91

Some people remember Andy North as the man who won two major tournaments in his career—the U.S. Open in 1978 and 1985.

Others know him, though, as the walking operating room. When it comes to health, Andy North's has continually gone south. Here's a list of the major ailments he's suffered:

- 1970: Left knee surgery
- 1983: Bone spur removed, right elbow
- 1986: Broken thumb
- 1987: Arthroscopic surgery, both knees
- 1988: Arthroscopic surgery, left knee
- 1989: Bone spur removed, neck
- 1989: Injured shoulder
- 1990: Arthroscopic surgery, left knee
- 1991: Four surgeries to remove skin cancer from nose and left cheek; plastic surgery to rebuild nose

Not included in the casualty list is a chronic bad back. "If I hadn't played when I was hurt," he said, "I wouldn't have teed it up in the last 20 years.

"It's become a joke in the locker room. Guys don't ask me, 'How was your winter?' They ask me, 'What kind of surgery did you have this past winter?' "

Ironically, it was an unusual ailment that first led North to golf. When he was in the seventh grade, a bone in his knee stopped growing and began disintegrating. North ended up on crutches for 18 months while his knee was repaired. Because he couldn't play his favorite sports of basketball and football, he took up golf. He became a star linksman in high school and college before turning pro.

Battered and bruised, North still tries to play. That is, when he isn't recovering from yet another surgery.

"Right now, I still spend two hours a day on rehab, every single day," he said. "Since 1985, all I've done is rehab."

Most Stitches Required After Strangling a Golf Club

6 stitches
Wayne Levi
1977 U.S. Open qualifier

Pro golfer Wayne Levi tried to choke his driver—and it retaliated!

At the U.S. Open qualifier in 1977, Levi needed only to finish with two pars on the final two holes to make it into the field for the biggest tournament of the year. On the 17th hole, he whacked a dreadful snap hook that flew out of bounds. Bogey was a certainty; double bogey was a definite possibility.

Levi was so angry that he gripped his hands around the neck of his driver and began to strangle it, shaking it in front of his face. Unfortunately, Levi shook it a little too hard. The shaft flexed and the head of the driver smacked him right in the mouth!

The impact loosened a tooth and cut his lip, and blood immediately began spurting down the front of his shirt. He hurriedly hustled to the scorer's tent where a doctor repaired the damage with six stitches.

The cut that was most important to Levi, though, wasn't the one on his lip. It was the tournament's—and Levi missed it.

Most Miles a Golf Writer Traveled in the Wrong Direction to Cover the Masters

1,070 miles
Bob Warters, 1992
Editor, Today's Golfer

Bob Warters, editor of the British magazine *Today's Golfer*, planned to fly from England to the Augusta National to cover the 1992 Masters. So he called his travel agent to book him on a flight to Augusta.

Everything went well on the first leg of the journey—a flight from Manchester, England, to Boston. After Warters cleared customs at the Boston airport, a friendly airline attendant looked at his ticket and pointed him to a nearby gate.

Warters boarded the plane and was a bit concerned when he noticed it was a prop and not a jet. Props are for short commuter hops. Augusta, Georgia, was more than 1,000 miles away. Oh, well, he thought. That's airline deregulation for you.

But Warters became even more concerned after the plane took off. He looked out his window and noticed something just wasn't right. "The ocean was on my right side, not my left," he said. "I surmised that we were headed north, but I figured it was just some quirk in the traffic pattern, that before long the pilot would turn around and get headed in the right direction."

But then the plane landed. Warters looked at his watch and noticed he had only been in the air for 50 minutes. The flight on a jetliner should have taken two hours. Something definitely wasn't right.

Warters went into the terminal and asked in his British accent, "Is this Augusta, Georgia?"

"No," came the reply. "You're in Augusta, Maine."

Aghast, Warters hustled back to the airline counter. He had to spend the night in Maine plus pay an extra $150 for a new plane ticket. But eventually he made his flight to Augusta, Georgia—in time to cover the Masters.

Most Feet a Golfer Has Sunk in a Bunker

5 feet
D.J. Bayly MacArthur, 1931
Rose Bay, New South Wales, Australia

D.J. Bayly MacArthur had that strange sinking feeling when he stepped into a bunker during a 1931 tournament in Rose Bay, New South Wales, Australia. The golfer was shocked to discover that he not only was stuck in the bunker but was actually sinking.

MacArthur, who weighed about 200 pounds, struggled to escape the clutches of the bunker, but couldn't get free. Desperately, he shouted for help as he sunk deeper and deeper. He was up to his armpits before help arrived and yanked him out.

An investigation revealed that the sand in the bunker had turned into deadly quicksand.

Most Legs Broken from Swinging a Club

1 leg
Richard Boxall
1991 British Open

English pro Richard Boxall was playing in the third round of the 1991 British Open at Royal Birkdale. He was only three shots off the pace and felt good about closing in on the leaders.

No sooner had he teed off than he collapsed in anguish on the ground, screaming in pain. At first no one knew what had happened, including Boxall. Spectators said they heard a loud crack as though a large branch had snapped.

What had snapped was Boxall's left leg. Incredibly, the force of his follow-through on his swing had somehow caused a fracture below the knee. Boxall was carted off the course in an ambulance and rushed to the hospital.

His freak mishap was one of the most serious golf course injuries ever experienced by a golfer during a major championship.

11

Wacky Money and Prize Records

Highest-Priced Cow Ever Won by a Pro

$5,000
Ian Baker-Finch
1988 Bridgestone/Aso Open

The most "udderly" ridiculous prize that pro Ian
Baker-Finch ever won on the golf course was a cow!

The Australian, who joined the PGA Tour in 1990,
knew he would receive some sort of bonus in addi-
tion to money for finishing first in the 1988 Bridge-
stone/Aso Open in Japan. He was expecting something like a car or free air travel.

"As I was standing on the 18th green at the end
of the tournament, one of the organizers led a cow
over to me," Baker-Finch recalled. "Aso is famous for
its beef and dairy products, and a local farming coop-
erative had donated this heifer as a prize."

At first, Baker-Finch didn't know what he was
going to do with a cow. "I suppose we could have cut
her up right then and had ourselves an Aussie bar-
becue," he joked.

Instead, the golfer conveniently sold the cow
back to the organizers for $5,000.

Biggest Winner's Check a Pro Attempted to Throw into the Fireplace

$45,000
Lanny Wadkins
1977 PGA Championship

When Lanny Wadkins won the 1977 PGA Championship—his first major—at Pebble Beach, he planned to
celebrate in a big way. It nearly cost him his entire
winnings.

After he collected his winner's check of $45,000 in a grand ceremony and spent an hour in the media room giving interviews, Wadkins returned to his swank hotel room with his wife, Penny.

Their room had been stocked with champagne and beer because the management believed Wadkins would be hosting a victory party. Nestled in front of the fireplace, Lanny and Penny began partying by themselves by having a glass or 10 of the bubbly.

"By the time nine o'clock rolled around, we were out in the street trying to hold each other up," recalled Wadkins. Realizing they were in no condition to go anywhere, the tipsy couple stumbled back into their room and immediately fell into a deep sleep.

"The next thing I remember was waking up around 4:00 A.M. because the room had gotten warm," Lanny said. "I got up and noticed a crumpled wad of paper on the floor. Yes, it was my check for $45,000. At some point during the night, I had tried to throw it into the fireplace. Thank God I missed.

"I carefully smoothed out the check and went back to bed," Wadkins recounted, adding that before falling back to sleep he said a little prayer of thanks for being too tipsy to hit the fire.

Most Prize Winnings Turned Down for Shooting an Ace

$90,000
Yoshiaka Ono
1981 Singapore Open

Seldom in golf history has there ever been a more perplexing dilemma than the one that faced Yoshiaka

Ono after he scored an ace on the 17th hole at the 1981 Singapore Open.

The dilemma? Whether to accept $50,000 in cash and a $40,000 car—the special bonus offered to anyone who made a hole in one on Number 17 during the event held at the Singapore Island Golf Club.

The 25-year-old Ono, who operated his father's electrical contracting business in Japan, was an amateur at the time of the shot. He was rejoicing over his great luck in winning the cash and car when someone reminded Ono that if he accepted the booty, he would become a professional. No longer could he participate in amateur events.

Although most scratch golfers would gladly give up their amateur status in exchange for accepting $90,000 in prize winnings, Ono was different. Cradling his head in his hands, the perplexed golfer sat in the locker room for three hours and tried to make a decision. He played golf for the love of the game and enjoyed competing in amateur events. Was it worth $90,000 in winnings to give that up?

Echoing the thoughts of many of his fellow competitors, a golfer walked over to Ono and declared, "Take it! The hell with being an amateur!"

Finally, Ono stood up and announced, "I don't want to be a professional. . . . But I'll never forget Singapore."

Least Amount of Money Pocketed After Winning a U.S. Open

$0.00
Gary Player
1965 U.S. Open

Gary Player didn't pocket a dime by winning the 1965 U.S. Open in an 18-hole playoff over Ken Nagle at Bellerive Country Club in St. Louis. When it came time to receive the winner's check of $25,000, Player declined to accept it personally, living up to a pledge he had made three years earlier.

In 1962, the South African pro vowed publicly that if he ever won a U.S. Open, he would give all the prize money to charity.

The $25,000 purse—worth over $100,000 by today's standards—represented a sizable increase over previous years, primarily because of golf's newly recognized television revenues. At the ceremony, Player announced that $5,000 would go to cancer research in honor of his father, who had died of the disease. The remaining $20,000 would go to the U.S. Golf Association for the promotion of junior golf.

"I always felt so fortunate to have the opportunity to play golf in the United States that I wanted to give something back to express my gratitude," Player said. "I think the United States has a wonderful program for junior golfers—something I would like to see in my country—and I will do whatever I can to promote it. This was just a small token of my appreciation for being allowed to support my family by playing golf in this country."

Actually, Player lost money by winning the U.S. Open. He gave his caddie $2,000 out of his own pocket, representing the 8 percent of the prize money that caddies normally receive.

Most Money Paid Out in One Day by a Resort to Golfers Who Collected on Their Snow Insurance Policy

$7,100
Sands Oceanfront, 1992
Myrtle Beach, South Carolina

When the Sands Oceanfront took out rain insurance for its golfing guests, the word *snow* was added to the policy as a joke. After all, this was Myrtle Beach, on the Atlantic Ocean, where it's not supposed to snow.

But it was no joke when a surprise two-inch snowfall hit in late January 1992. Forty-eight golfers at the hotel presented management with the paid-up insurance policies. The total tab to the resort was $7,100.

Most Money Won by a College Golfer with One Swing of His Club

$1 million
Jason Bohn, 1992
Harry Pritchett Golf Course
University of Alabama
Tuscaloosa, Alabama

With one swing of his club, University of Alabama golfer Jason Bohn lost his collegiate eligibility and his amateur status. But he didn't mind. That's because he pocketed a cool $1 million by sinking an ace.

Bohn, a 19-year-old sophomore chemistry major from Mifflinburg, Pennsylvania, was competing in the 1992 Hole 'N One Shootout—a charity event to raise money for renovation of Tuscaloosa's historic Jemison House mansion. After a preliminary round, each of 12 finalists had a one-shot chance at the million bucks if he could ace the 135-yard second hole at the college's Harry Pritchett Golf Course.

With his 9-iron, Bohn lofted the ball onto the green where it landed to the left of the cup, bounced twice—and rolled right into the hole. And suddenly Bohn—a walk-on hoping to win a scholarship on the golf team—was an instant millionaire. He will pocket an annual check of $50,000 for 20 years.

But there was a price to pay. By accepting the prize money, Bohn had to quit the Crimson Tide golf team because he was now considered a professional. "I was looking forward to playing," he said. "I think I'm going to really miss being on the team. But it didn't take me long to decide what I was going to do. This is a once-in-a-lifetime opportunity."

Minutes after nailing his million-dollar ace, Bohn called his father, James, back in Mifflinburg and told him, "I have some good news and some bad news. The bad news is I'm no longer on the golf team. The good news is I'm now the fourth highest money winner on the PGA Tour."

Most Money Won by a Pro Thanks to a Phone Call

$7,733
Bob Goalby, 1970
Las Vegas, Nevada

Bob Goalby had a fitful time at the 1970 Sahara Invitational, struggling along on an easy course to shoot 71-75 in the first two rounds. Fully expecting to miss the cut because of such mediocre scores, Goalby walked into the locker room, packed his bags, and headed to the airport.

Eventually he heard the boarding call and got on the plane. But while sitting in his seat waiting to pull away from the gate, he began thinking. He looked out the window and saw the wind had picked up considerably. Then he remembered how bumpy the greens had been that day. Maybe, just maybe, the scores are going to be higher than I anticipated, he thought.

Goalby hustled off the plane and ran to a pay phone. To his surprise, he learned he had made the cut.

Given a reprieve, Goalby frantically retrieved his clubs and luggage and caught a cab back to the hotel. Instead of moping at home over the next two days, he played in the tournament. And as luck would have it, he caught a hot streak, shooting a pair of 66s in the final two rounds.

As a result, Goalby finished in a tie for second and was presented with a check for $7,733—money earned thanks to a last-second, 10-cent phone call.

Most Years a Tour Pro Was Sponsored by a Band Leader

3 years
Gary McCord, 1974–77

When Gary McCord graduated from Qualifying School, he quickly realized two facts: he couldn't afford to support himself on the Tour, but he knew a very wealthy neighbor who could.

Famed band leader Lawrence Welk lived down the block from McCord's family in Escondido, California. There was one problem, however. McCord had never actually met Welk. But that didn't stop him from placing a telephone call to Welk's business agent, just in case there might be interest.

McCord was delighted a few weeks later when he received a call from Welk, who offered a proposal: Welk would sponsor McCord for three years. In return, McCord would represent Welk's Country Club Village, a mobile home park with an 18-hole, par-3 golf course. McCord readily agreed.

A month later, at Welk's invitation, McCord appeared on the band leader's TV show. To the young golfer's surprise, Welk asked McCord to hit a ball at an archery target 35 feet away. Shaking like a leaf— and praying he wouldn't embarrass himself—McCord wowed the audience when he hit the target with a 4-iron.

Shortest Time to Win a New Truck in a Golf Tournament

10 seconds
Bob Heath, 1992
Deercroft Golf & Country Club
Wagram, North Carolina

At a charity fund-raiser at Deercroft, a new GMC truck was being offered to the first person to make an ace on the 12th hole. It was a shotgun-start tournament, meaning foursomes would start on all 18 holes at once. Bob Heath began the tournament at Number 12.

He was playing for the first time with a new set of Ping irons. He removed the plastic from his 7-iron, stepped up to the ball, and swatted it. It flew in for a hole in one, and Heath drove home with his new set of irons in a brand-new truck.

Most Money Paid for a Round That Could Have Been Free

$40
Scott Gaertner, 1992
Stonecreek, The Golf Club
Paradise Valley, Arizona

Stonecreek, The Golf Club tried a promotion to increase business during the slow summer months. It tried to lure golfers with an offer they absolutely couldn't refuse—a round that would cost whatever they felt like paying!

Taking advantage of the one-day-only promotion were 138 golfers, including 34 who had never played Stonecreek before. When each golfer finished the round, which normally cost $20, he chose how much to pay and filled out an evaluation sheet of the course.

Scott Gaertner, a Scottsdale resident, paid $40 for the greens fee, the most of any golfer that day. He said his experience was well worth the money because "the course was in the best shape I've ever seen."

One golfer paid nothing, but that was no reflection on the course. He said he thought his round was worth $25, but because it was his 50th birthday, he treated himself to a day of free golf.

Surprisingly, the promotion may have backfired. The average amount paid for greens fees was $16.12, nearly $4 less than the normal summer weekday rate. Attendance of 138 golfers was down from the normal total on summer Mondays of 192. "When we tell people what to pay, we get more players than when we allow them to pay whatever they want," said Stonecreek marketing director Mike Petty.

Most Cadillacs Won by an Amateur Golfer in the Same Event

2 Cadillacs
Ross Applegate, 1976–77
Del Webb Sahara Tahoe Tournament

Days before playing in the 1976 Del Webb Sahara Tahoe Tournament, real estate salesman Ross Applegate, of San Jose, California, bought a Cadillac, which he and his wife, Patricia, drove to the event.

He could have saved the money he spent on the car.

Playing the Incline Village Golf Course's par-3 15th hole, which featured a closest-to-the-hole prize, Applegate swung his 8-iron and left his shot just 23 inches away from the cup. It was the hole's best tee shot of the day, so Applegate was given the keys to a new Cadillac.

Since his "old" one still seemed to be running just fine after three days out of the showroom, Applegate sold the car he had just won. He went home with $9,500 instead of the Cadillac.

A year later, Applegate returned for the same event. Again he won the closest-to-the-pin hole, cozying his tee shot to within three feet of Edgewood Tahoe's seventh hole. The prize was another new Cadillac.

Nope, he told tourney officials, he still didn't need a new Caddy. So he sold the car to the sponsoring casino and walked away with $8,400 in cash.

Most Fattening Endorsement Contract Signed by a Pro

500 Whoppers
Howard Twitty, 1977

PGA Tour pro Howard Twitty is a very big guy, standing 6'5" tall. And he loves hamburgers—so much so that in 1977 he negotiated a small contract with Burger King to display its logo on his bag.

Because Twitty was 51st on the PGA money list at the time, it was an extremely small transaction. Forget the money, he told Burger King. The deal he finally settled on was for 500 free Whoppers. Presumably, they weren't all consumed at one sitting.

Most Bonus Money Missed Out on After Making Two Aces

$20,000
Trevor McDonald
1991 Victorian Open

Golfers at the Victorian Open in Melbourne, Australia, had a chance to win a $20,000 bonus for making a certain hole in one.

Australian teaching pro Trevor McDonald astounded fellow competitors and the gallery by nailing two holes in one in the opening round. He drilled one ace at the fifth hole and the other at the 17th.

Unfortunately for McDonald, he didn't collect one cent of the $20,000. The bonus money was only for someone who aced the *11th* hole.

12

Outrageous Miscellaneous Records

Most Consecutive Holes a Pro Coughed During His Opponents' Swings

17 holes
Seve Ballesteros
1991 Ryder Cup

Seve Ballesteros had a bad case of "sandpaper throat" that rubbed his opponents the wrong way.

Ballesteros and Jose Maria Olazabal teamed up in the opening match of the 1991 Ryder Cup against Americans Paul Azinger and Chip Beck at Kiawah Island, South Carolina. Azinger and Beck were three-up at the nine-hole turn, but the Spaniards won five of the next eight holes to close out the Yanks after the 17th.

Azinger blamed the loss on a distracting habit of Ballesteros's—a constant clearing of his throat whenever the Americans were about to hit. "Believe me, guys, he [Ballesteros] is the king of gamesmanship," Azinger told the press after the match. "He knows every trick in the book."

"That's ridiculous," said Ballesteros. "I just had a bad cold acting up in the chilly ocean air."

The next morning, Ballesteros and Olazabal were scheduled to play Fred Couples and crusty veteran Raymond Floyd. Just as Couples was about to hit his tee shot on the first hole, Ballesteros's cold acted up again, and he loudly cleared his throat.

Floyd walked directly up to Ballesteros, put his nose an inch from Ballesteros's face, and glared at him eyeball to eyeball. Not a word was exchanged, nor was there need for one. Incredibly, Ballesteros's cold didn't bother him the rest of the day. By the way, the Spanish "hacker" and his partner still managed to beat Floyd and Couples 3 and 2.

Most Yards a Donkey Ran with a Golf Ball

50 yards
Middleton, County Cork, Ireland, 1922

Michael McEvoy made golf's most asinine shot.

McEvoy's drive from the third tee went right into the ear of a donkey that was grazing on the fairway.

The stunned ass stood still for a moment. But when McEvoy got within a few yards of the animal, it took off. About 50 yards into the rough, the donkey shook his head and the ball fell out. The ball was so deep in the woods that McEvoy took a double-bogey six.

Youngest Fan to Interrupt the British Open by Running Nude on the Fairway

16 years old
Unidentified streaker, 1991

During the opening round of the British Open, a 16-year-old blonde in the gallery tore off all her clothes. Then she ducked under the ropes, sprinted down the fairway, and caught up with Jose Maria Olazabal on the first green. The young Spaniard tried to avoid her, but the streaker managed to throw her arms around the stunned golfer and give him a hug.

After admitting he had lost his composure, a shaken Olazabal said afterward, "By the time I got to my ball, I was OK." Then, trying to act cool, he added, "It was just a naked woman, that's all."

Surprisingly, the young woman was accompanied to the tournament by her mother, who told reporters that her daughter had "always had a mind of her own." The teenager, whom police refused to name because she was a minor, was corralled by marshals who quickly led her off the green. She asked one of the officials for his R&A sweater to cover up with, but he declined. However, a man came down from the grandstand and gave her his raincoat.

Said Nick Price, who was playing with Olazabal, "I've never been so shocked in my life."

Most Unusual Burial Place for a Golfer

The 17th hole
William K. Garner, 1967
Croham Hurst Golf Club
England

167
....

William K. Garner was a golf fanatic who lived to play the game. He always said that when he died, he wanted to spend eternity on the links.

He passed away in 1967 at the age of 75. So, according to his wishes, his friends took his ashes to the Croham Hurst Golf Club. There his fellow club members followed out his wishes, but with one final little prank of their own. They scattered his ashes over the area of the 17th hole where he had spent most of his time—130 yards out and in the rough!

Oldest Woman to Play on the LPGA Tour

400 years old (approximately)
Muffin Spencer-Devlin

Pro golfer Muffin Spencer-Devlin, a firm believer in reincarnation, says that in an earlier life she was a 16th-century Japanese woman.

"I know that's true," she said. "The first time I went over to Japan, I had that déjà vu feeling. I'd been there before. The rains, the mists, the temples—everything seemed so familiar."

Spencer-Devlin was so moved by the experience that she immersed herself in the Japanese culture. She attended a language school to study Japanese and now speaks it fluently.

Spencer-Devlin competes in 10 tournaments a year in Japan, where she also regularly appears on TV talk shows. Her command of Japanese made her a natural for providing the Japanese translation on teacher Bob Toski's TV golf show, filmed in the country for Japanese audiences.

Not surprisingly, her best friend on the LPGA Tour is Ayako Okamoto, the most popular female athlete in Japan.

First Reference to Golf as a Health Benefit

1772
Sermons to Gentlemen About Temperance and Exercise
University of Notre Dame Library

In a 1772 book entitled *Sermons to Gentlemen About Temperance and Exercise* is the first known published remark about the sport's health benefits: "Man would live 10 years longer for using this exercise once or twice a week."

The book was written by Dr. Benjamin Bush, a Philadelphian who had studied medicine at the University of Edinburgh and been exposed to golf in Scotland.

Most Miles Traveled Only to Be DQ'ed on the First Hole

4,500 miles
Fred Rowland
1988 British Amateur Championship
Porthcawl, Wales

After spending months of practise and raising thousands of dollars, Kansas City golfer Fred Rowland eagerly flew 4,500 miles to Wales to play in the biggest tournament of his life—the 1988 British Amateur.

169

On the big day, he was ready; he was psyched. As expected, the weather was miserable, with rain driven by 30-mile-an-hour winds.

After standing in the rain for an hour waiting to tee off, Rowland, holding an umbrella blown inside out, heeded nature's call. He ran over to a portable lavatory about 100 yards away. Because he had to take off his rain suit and then put it back on, he spent a little longer than expected.

When he came toddling back to the tee, he saw one of his playing partners teeing off. Rowland was waiting to hit next. But the head official, Sir Michael Reese, informed him that since Rowland wasn't at the tee when his name was called, he had been disqualified.

All the practise and money; all his hopes and dreams were dashed—all because of a trip to the bathroom. "What's really upsetting," Rowland recalled, "was that I didn't really have to go to the bathroom that badly."

Oldest Golfer to Shoot His Age

103 years old
Arthur Thompson, 1973
Uplands Golf Course
Ontario, Canada

Arthur Thompson was the Methuselah of the links.

The hale and hearty Canadian was still playing golf competitively on his 103rd birthday in 1973. On that day, Thompson became the oldest man in history to equal his age on the golf course by shooting an amazing 103 at Uplands Golf Course in Ontario, Canada, near his home.

Being the oldest linksman was old hat for Thompson. For nearly a decade, he remained the oldest man to have bettered his age, shooting in the 90s on several occasions.

Thompson scored in the 70s more than 100 times while he was in his 80s. At the age of 89, he shot a round of 82. When he was well into his 90s, Thompson was hitting drives that traveled more than 200 yards. All of his best scores were shot at Uplands, a challenging course measuring more than 6,215 yards.

Shortly before his death in 1975 at the age of 105, he still enjoyed playing nine holes.

Most Caddies Fired By a Pro in a Major Tournament

4 caddies
Sam Snead
1946 British Open
St. Andrews, Scotland

At the 1946 British Open, Sam Snead went through the St. Andrews' caddies like a bucket of range balls. He had to fire four of them because they deliberately tried to sabotage his game.

They were miffed over an offhand remark made by the country-bred West Virginian on his first trip to Scotland. While heading to the Open on a train from London, Snead spotted a run-down, weedy fairway in the midst of some craggy moors and said to a fellow passenger, "Say, that looks like an old, abandoned golf course. What did they call it?"

The passenger, a well-dressed English gentleman, gasped, "My good sir! That is the Royal and Ancient Club of St. Andrews, founded in 1754! And it is not now, nor ever will be, abandoned!"

"Holy smoke, I'm sorry," said Snead. "Down home we wouldn't plant cow beets on land like that."

When word reached the British press that Snead had maligned the most famous links in the world, the newspapers condemned him. St. Andrews' caddies then made life miserable for Snead during the first three days of the Open.

The first caddie tried to annoy Snead by whistling between his teeth whenever the golfer putted. The bag-lugger further vexed Snead by wiping the ball clean with the same rag the caddie used to blow his nose.

Snead replaced him with a caddie who deliberately gave him the wrong yardage and clubs. Once again, Snead demanded that the caddie master find him a new bag-toter. The golfer was given a caddie who had been found sleeping in a bunker. He was useless. He failed to make the starting time because he got drunk the night before and wound up in jail.

Snead's fourth caddie lasted a round before he was fired for demanding more money.

The fifth caddie stuck with Snead for the rest of the tournament—only after Snead bribed him with £20 to keep his mouth shut and nose clean.

Despite all his caddie troubles, Snead won the Open by four strokes. When Snead walked off the green with the victory, his caddie told him, "I'd like to have the ball. I've never caddied for a champion in my life." After Snead graciously handed him the ball, the caddie beamed with joy and gushed, "I'll treasure it for the rest of my life."

The next morning, Snead learned that his caddie had sold the treasured ball for £50.

Oldest Golfer to Reach the Finals of an Important Match Play Tournament

78 years old
F.L. Callender
1932 Jubilee Vase
St. Andrews, Scotland

F. L. Callender, formerly of St. Andrews, was the oldest golfer ever to reach the finals of an important match play tournament.

In 1932, at the age of 78, Callender shocked the local citizenry by winning a remarkable eight consecutive matches in his quest for the coveted Jubilee Vase. The trophy was awarded to the winner of the grueling match play competition at the Old Course at St. Andrews.

Although Callender was defeated in the finals, 4 and 2, his was the most impressive performance by a septuagenarian in top-level competition until nearly 60 years later when 75-year-old Jerry Barber nearly won a Senior PGA Tour event.

Most Yards a Golf Ball Traveled After Being Hit Out of a Beer Bottle in a Major Tournament

25 yards
Harry Bradshaw
1949 British Open
Royal St. George's, England

Harry Bradshaw might have won the 1949 British Open if only he had decided to stay away from the bottle. Don't get the wrong impression. He didn't drink from the bottle; he hit it.

But his thinking couldn't have been any worse had he taken a nip or two before the first tee.

In the second round, the chubby Irishman was just one shot off the pace when his drive on the fifth hole veered into the rough—and bounced right into a broken beer bottle. The bottle was standing upright with the neck and shoulder broken off and jagged edges sticking up.

After 15 minutes of studying the situation, Bradshaw chose to play the bottle and ball. He boldly reached for his blaster, closed his eyes to protect them from flying glass, and swung with all his might. The bottle splintered into dangerous shards that flew in all directions. But the ball moved only 25 yards. Shaken by the unlucky incident, Bradshaw took a double-bogey six on the hole and finished the round with a shaky 77.

He regained his fine golfing form in the final two rounds and wound up in a playoff, which he then lost to South African Bobby Locke.

Had Bradshaw sought a ruling instead of hitting away, he could have treated the bottle as an obstruction and moved it without penalty. "If I had sent for a ruling," he later admitted, "I might have won the championship."

Most Errant Drives Hit Before Breaking Out in Song

5 errant drives
Johnny Mathis, 1970
Moor Allerton
Yorkshire, England

Singer Johnny Mathis was playing golf at Moor Allerton in Yorkshire, with some British companions when he faltered badly on the eighth hole.

He socked his drive out of bounds. His second tee shot soared over the trees out of sight. His third drive went even farther, and was never seen again.

Muttering to himself, Mathis determinedly teed up another ball, only to send that to bye-bye land. His fifth ball tailed off into a bush, but at least it could be recovered.

As his group walked down the fairway, Mathis lagged behind. Suddenly, his smooth, silky voice filled the air as he sang the musical scale, ending triumphantly on the highest note. When his playing partners wheeled around in wonder, Mathis told them, "Thank God I can still sing."

Most Accurate Drive by a Hung-Over Pro during a Tournament

Christy O'Connor, 1963
World Cup
St. Nom la Breteche, France

Colorful Irish pro Christy O'Connor, Jr., found himself in a predicament at the 1963 World Cup at St. Nom la Breteche near Paris. It was nearly tee time and he could barely see—because, as he later admitted, he was terribly hung over from partying the night before.

He was roused in the locker room by Mark Wilson, the golf correspondent for the *Daily Express*. Wilson informed the bleary-eyed O'Connor that his tee time was imminent and he might want to put his shoes on and make his way to the first tee. O'Connor reluctantly staggered to his feet and told Wilson to get a large mug of black coffee. "Pace off 65 yards from the 200-yard post on the first hole and wait for me there in the woods," the golfer said.

Wilson got the coffee and headed for the woods, while O'Connor stumbled off to the tee. When his turn came to hit, Christy launched a 265-yard drive into the woods. Wilson watched the ball rattle around in the trees and drop a few feet from where he stood.

Moments later, O'Connor arrived. The Irishman chugged the coffee, thanked his friend, and pressed on. Christy managed to shoot three under par that day—a remarkable score given the circumstances.

Worst Score on a Hole in a Major Tournament in Modern History

15
Hermann Tissies
1950 British Open
Troon Golf Links
Scotland

Flailing away in the bunkers like no other British Open competitor had ever done before, Hermann Tissies recorded the highest single-hole score in modern Open history—a bungling 15. What made this black mark even more inglorious was that he qaudruple-triple bogeyed the shortest hole on the course.

On Troon's 127-yard, par-3 eighth hole—noted for its tiny green known as the "Postage Stamp"—Tissies got his worst licking ever.

His tee shot plopped into one of the three pot bunkers that guard the green. Tissies blasted out of the bunker only to land in another. He pitched out, but then shanked his next shot back into a third bunker. From there, he swung four times without getting the ball out. Finally, on his ninth shot of the hole, he banged it out of the trap—smack into the second bunker. Then he pitched the ball right back into the first bunker.

Tissies managed to explode out of the bunker and onto the fringe of the green. He was so rattled that he three-putted for his mortifying score of 15 and finished the round with a deplorable 92.

The Scotsman, called Tissie's disaster "a horrible species of ping-pong played between the bunkers."